# FOUL DEEDS & SUSPICIOUS DEATHS IN & AROUND THE FENS

*Map of Cambridgeshire, 1809.* Cambridgeshire Archives

Foul Deeds & Suspicious Deaths In & Around

# THE FENS

## GLENDA GOULDEN

**Wharncliffe Books**

**First Published in Great Britain in 2008 by**
**Wharncliffe Books**
*an imprint of*
**Pen and Sword Books Ltd.**
**47 Church Street**
**Barnsley**
**South Yorkshire**
**S70 2AS**

Copyright © Glenda Goulden 2008

ISBN: 978-1-84563-072-0

Typeset in 10/12pt Plantin by Concept, Huddersfield.

Printed and bound in England by
CPI UK.

Pen & Sword Books Ltd incorporates the Imprints of Pen
& Sword Aviation, Pen & Sword Maritime, Pen & Sword
Military, Wharncliffe Local History, Pen & Sword Select,
Pen & Sword Military Classics, Leo Cooper, Remember
When, Seaforth Publishing and Frontline Publishing.

For a complete list of Pen & Sword titles please contact
PEN & SWORD BOOKS LIMITED
47 Church Street
Barnsley
South Yorkshire
S70 2BR
England
E-mail: enquiries@pen-and-sword.co.uk
Website: www.pen-and-sword.co.uk

# Contents

# Acknowledgements

This work was made possible by the excellent research facilities available at local studies archives, libraries and museums in and around the Fens and the informed interest of their staff, most notably at Downham Market, Ely, King's Lynn, Lincoln, Littleport, March, Northampton, Peterborough, Whittlesey and Wisbech, and at the University Library and Squire Law Library, Cambridge. Especial appreciation goes to Chris Jakes and Sue Slack of the Cambridgeshire Collection, Cambridge Central Library.

# Introduction

Diarist Samuel Pepys, forced into the Fens in pursuit of an inheritance in the autumn of 1663, thought the area around Wisbech 'a heathen place' where he was 'bit cruelly by the gnatts'. Celia Fiennes, an early travel writer riding around Britain in 1698, had even worse luck in Ely. She found it 'ye dirtiest place I ever saw' and 'tho my chamber was near twenty stepps up I had froggs and slow-worms and snailes in my roome'.

The Fens were known to be unhealthy and yet, because of their uniqueness, adventurous authors were drawn there through the sixteenth and seventeenth centuries to make tours and travels and then to write of the foulness they had found. In 1722, with less disapproval, Daniel Defoe saw the Isle of Ely 'wrapped up in blankets' of Michaelmas fogs with the lantern of the cathedral only now and then to be seen above, but he did call the Fens 'the sink of no less than thirteen counties', and listed them. One after another the curious came and had to 'avoyd the divellish stinging of the Gnatts' which brought agues and malarial fevers. It was a brave outsider who ventured into the watery, muddy, malodorous flatness of the most unwholesome place in Britain, and yet so many did, and went on doing so. They always had.

Over the centuries, wave after wave of invaders sought the fenland waterways and the habitable islands amongst them – the Romans, the Anglo Saxons, the Vikings and the Normans. They came and went. They may have attempted to make the fenlands drier in part – when and where crops could be grown the land was fertile – but they all left them much as they had found them.

The same higher land above the flat wet drew the monastic orders to build great abbeys and monasteries as well as many smaller religious houses. The Fens may have been, to most people, a God-forsaken wasteland, but at such as Crowland, Thorney, Ramsey, Ely and Peterborough, the religious found an isolated nearness to their God – until Henry came along with his Dissolution in the 1530s.

The Fens were often a place of refuge to those who challenged authority, such as Hereward the Wake, and a challenge to be overcome by kings and would-be kings. Canute, who thought that he could command water, tried his hand in the fenlands, as did Kings John and Charles, and Oliver Cromwell.

Charles I planned to build an 'eminent town' in the Fens, but it was destined never to be. Charlemont was to have been built at Manea, near Ely, with a canal to connect it to the Great Ouse, and he hoped to drain the wetness, joining with the Adventurers in their first serious attempt to do so.

Oliver Cromwell realised the advantages of a dry fenland, but he was against the land grab being made by those financing the draining. After the Civil War, he would be a chief advocate for the completion of the work of the Earl of Bedford, but he was a champion for the rights of the fenmen – until he lost his head. One of the drainers sized him up exactly in 1653 with, 'I am tould that my Lord Generall Cromwell should saye the drayninge of the fens was a good work, but that the drayners had too great a proportion of the land ... and that the poore were not enough provided for.'

The 'poore' thought so too. The fen people were an independent race of stilt walkers, punters and skaters, living by fishing, wildfowling and farming their summer-dry land, and they were content doing so. Previous attempts at draining had never amounted to much, but now they faced the possibility of losing their land and their livelihood. So, though fated to lose, they fought it. Their fighting against the unwanted incomers of the seventeenth century, the first successful drainers under the Dutchman Cornelius Vermuyden, earned them the name that was to last to the present day – fen tigers.

Emerging from the wetness harnessed by Vermuyden was what was to become the richest farmland in Britain. Eventually, there would be 700,000 acres of it, from the silt fens of Lincolnshire to the black peat fens of Cambridgeshire and on into Norfolk, a flat vastness of land beneath an enormity of sky.

How small was man as he went about the business of living, and of dying, there. The Fens have always been a different place. After the draining it became a changed world, the land shrinking in level as the peat dried, but still like nowhere else in Britain. Its people, the fen tigers, the yellowbellies, the fen slodgers, remained the same at heart. Their way of life may have changed, the land dominating their existence as before the water had, but they were the same hardy, stubborn, insular breed that Cromwell had backed.

The crimes taking place in and around the Fens seem strangely fitted to the world in which they were committed. Most have a frisson of singularity that seems to set them in and around the fenlands of East Anglia.

This retelling of some of the crimes which have taken place there through more than two hundred years begins with murder in Whittlesey. Two of the small market town's inhabitants were sentenced to death in 1749, a wife who had poisoned her husband with arsenic and a husband who had cut his wife's throat with a razor. He asked that he might see her burned at the stake in Ely before he kept his own appointment with the hangman.

Over a hundred years later, in 1863, Whittlesey was rocked by another murder, the horrific burning alive of a prostitute at one of the town's maltings, as exciting an event as the 1851 pumping dry of Whittlesey Mere, a 3000 acre lake, the last of many in the Fens. Crowds watched the surfacing of gasping shoals of fish, the bones of a killer whale, and lost silver from Ramsey Abbey.

The less wet fens made farm labourers of the people, women as well as men working in the fields. But life was wretched, with illness and poverty widespread. They had more to worry about than the gnats!

In 1816, after the end of the Napoleonic Wars, there was unemployment, low wages and high food prices. With acres of wheat growing around them, the men were forced to riot to make their plight known and to steal the bread to feed their families. Two Downham Market rioters were hung at Norwich and five Littleport rioters at Ely.

Grievances still smouldered, leading to incendiarism and the breaking of farm machinery. Farm buildings and stacks burned through the three counties with one fire, at March in 1833, having tragic consequences for the sister of one of the young arsonists. As tragic as the outcome for a farm labourer as, in defiance of the Game Laws, he went poaching with an associate on the Norfolk–Cambridgeshire border.

Throughout the nineteenth century, many fen dwellers became addicted to opium, then easily available. It eased the pain and the miseries of life – but how easy to overdose a baby or child, accidentally of course. Here are told the poignant stories of some of the cases of death involving opiates which reached the courts, deaths in which the women of the various fenland communities were closely involved.

As easily come by as opium was arsenic. It was chosen by so many nineteenth century poisoners in Britain that the Arsenic Act of 1851 was introduced, along with the poison book and the colouring of the arsenic to make it unlike sugar, in an effort to control its use. It was the first legal restriction on the sale of a poison after a decade of concern, spearheaded by the new Pharmaceutical Society. But it remained available – as a vermin killer. That, and the appropriately named cut-throat razor, feature here in killings in Wisbech and Horncastle in 1861 and Peterborough in 1914. One Lincolnshire wife used strychnine, the cruellest poison of all, to kill her husband in 1934. She became the last person to be hung at Hull Prison, which it is said she has haunted ever since. They make gruesome reading.

Into the twentieth century, the richest crop growing area in Britain was only kept dry by a network of drains, channels, dykes and rivers, and by continual pumping on a vast scale. But even so, as in 1947, floods happened from time to time. The farmer still relied on the work of others to keep the waters at bay as he worked his land with its far horizons.

But, remote as many fenland farms are, violent death has still stalked their dark acres, two farmers, in 1956 and 1961, being clubbed to death in acts of robbery, jealousy and theft. A third farmer was the killer, pulling the trigger to shoot dead the man who was taking his land from him.

Policing of the isolated communities in fenland has not been easy although, in the early decades of the nineteenth century, there was a reliable constable in each area and there is evidence of liaison between constables, even across county boundaries. They worked so well that there was opposition to the formation of the professional Norfolk Rural Police in 1839. Critics said that, unlike the constable in each community, it would be 'a moveable rambling police which no-one will ever know where to find'. But it was formed, and much mileage had to be walked, with the only advice given to Downham Market men being to 'make the best of it', advice taken to heart by one officer, disciplined soon after the force's foundation, for 'working his beat with his arms round the waist of a woman'.

But the crimes involving police officers which are retold here took place in urban areas in the twentieth century. In Ely, in 1930, a popular sergeant, wounded in the First World War, lost his career and his reputation over 'a serious charge' and in Peterborough in 1961 an inspector died in a stabbing – but was soon back on duty.

The Second World War, and the need to feed a nation at war, saw the Fens increasing food production to new heights as every scrap of land was put to the plough. As a ring of airfields operated round the fen edges, the men working the land, given the task of looking for enemy agents parachuting into the area, leapt at the chance to fight Mr Hitler in their own way. And they did find the enemy in the Fens.

To be born in the Fens in the nineteenth century was a chancy business. Countless numbers of babies and small children died, many of them illegitimate, as they were fed opiates. But one illegitimate

*Fenland landscape, Downham Market.* The author

baby, in 1930, needed no poison. She was found floating in a cardboard box in the river Nene at March. As sad an end as that of an adored seven-year-old boy as Christmas Day ended in Downham Market in 1972. He got his mother 'all worked up'. Children do that to mothers, but not usually with death as the consequence.

*River Great Ouse and Fen, Ely.* The Author

The crimes that you will read about here show that a grimy, populous conurbation was not needed for foul deeds to have their way. Death walks anywhere. The solitary labourer, a distant speck as he worked his far acres, was as likely, when differences in population levels were considered, to be a victim as any city dweller, the fen town shopkeeper was as likely to sell death, and the fen baby was more likely to breathe its last before its first birthday.

Evil stalked the Fens and always, all around, was the harshness and the beauty of life close to the earth, an earth that seemed to spin away and, at night, become one with the stars.

Chapter 1

# A Life at Stake
# 1748–1749

I t still happens. A parent does not approve of their child's choice of partner. It may be that an adoring father cannot accept the idea of any man carrying away his daughter. But, sometimes, it is one particular young man that he cannot take to. There is just something about him . . .

And that is what happened with Amy Conquest of Whittlesey in 1748. She fell in love with Thomas Reed, a butcher, and her father did not like him.

Headstrong Amy stood up to her father and continued walking out with Reed. Certain that they were to marry and very much in love, she consented to intimacy. And then, in the summer of 1748, when Amy was barely nineteen, he told her that he was leaving Whittlesey to find work in London. But he would be back soon, and they would get married.

Amy felt abandoned. She had given him her all and that was how he treated her. When he did not return as quickly as she expected she turned to 'I'll show him' tactics and began to respond to the attentions of John Hutchinson, an Irishman who had been in Whittlesey for about a year and a half. She had known of his interest while she was courting Thomas Reed, but she had kept him at a distance. Now – well – Reed had left her, hadn't he!

She did not like Hutchinson, but it was a reassurance to know that he was attracted to her and wanted her, and he was there, in Whittlesey. Thomas Conquest too, now that he seemed to have been proved right by the feckless Reed's desertion, found Hutchinson a much more pleasing prospect for his daughter.

Amy underwent, without enjoyment, a brief courtship, and then, on 24 August, Hutchinson asked her father for his consent to their marriage. He agreed at once and the wedding was arranged for the next day. It was not Amy's marriage that Conquest was opposed to – at that time it was an economic necessity for a woman to be married –

*Market Street, Whittlesey, today.* The author

but her marriage to Reed. For some reason, he was not the man he wanted Amy to be associated with. She was very young and perhaps not very worldly, unable to see beyond the physical attraction to judge Thomas Reed's real worth. Whatever Conquest's reason, he did not like him and he welcomed John Hutchinson as Amy's saviour. They would marry the next day. As quickly as that.

But why the rush? It is possible that Conquest had discovered that Thomas Reed was not in London, if he ever had been. He was not far from Whittlesey and was, in fact, on his way back there. Thomas Reed was so close to Whittlesey that, hurriedly as the wedding had been arranged, he got to hear of it. He raced back to the town, but just minutes too late. He arrived to see Amy leaving the church as John Hutchinson's bride.

Poor Amy. She realised at once what a mistake she had made. If only she had waited a little bit longer instead of becoming the wife of a man she did not love. The moment she set eyes on Reed again her love for him flared into flame. He was the one. Almost as soon as she had cast aside whatever finery she had found to wear for such a hasty wedding they began to see each other, so openly that there was gossip.

John Hutchinson knew what was going on. They argued about it, but Amy said that her affair with Reed would go on. She refused to end it even though Hutchinson, not a man to have his wife cuckold him, began to attack her physically. When the beatings did not persuade her to end her affair he turned to ale, a solace.

Living together became unbearable and very quickly Amy began to think of how she might get free of her marriage. And what came to mind was poison. She would poison Hutchinson. Deadly poisons, notably strychnine and arsenic, were easily come by. At a time when hygiene and sanitation were primitive, homes became overrun with mice and rats and both poisons were available from shops and druggists for use against vermin. Arsenic was the most popular choice because it was almost tasteless and could be mixed with meal or grain to make an appetising rat or mouse poison. Amy bought arsenic for use against vermin of a different kind.

When they had been married for seven long, tormented weeks, her husband complained one morning of aches and pains. It was mid-October and painful joints were common in Whittlesey as the autumn mists began to roll in over the fen and damp to rise from the mere. That was Amy's opportunity.

She warmed some ale for him. She said it would do him good. He drank it and said that he felt no better for it. In fact, he felt much worse. Amy's sister, Ann, was concerned when she saw the state of him and sent for Mary Watson, a local woman with nursing skills, while Amy left the house, unable to bear seeing her poor dear husband so poorly. His condition continued to worsen and, after hours of agony, he died the same day.

Relying mainly on the evidence of Mary Watson, who said that Hutchinson had not made any comment to her that he had been poisoned, and as she had laid him out she had seen nothing to make her doubt that he had died of natural causes, it was decided that there had been nothing amiss. The symptoms of arsenic poisoning could be very much like those of food poisoning, a fact which must have helped many a murderer. It helped Amy Hutchinson.

John Hutchinson was buried in Whittlesey on 16 October, two days after his death, and all was well. Amy had got away with murder. She was a little older than when she had first flaunted her affair with Thomas Reed, but she was no wiser. As soon as Hutchinson was beneath the sod she and Reed began an open relationship. There was shock at Amy's blatant lack of respect as Reed moved into the marital home with her. The town's upholders of the law and of all that was right and proper could not fail to be aware of the accusations rumbling through Whittlesey. They knew their duty. They took action at once.

Hutchinson's body was exhumed on 19 October and a post-mortem was held by three surgeons – John Clarke, John Stona and William Benning. Forensics were of the most basic, but they could be effective. In that case they were. The body was opened and the stomach contents, which were seen to be bloodied, as if some corrosive substance had been ingested, were fed to a dog. The dog died within hours and, when its stomach was opened, the same bloody mess was found. That was taken as proof enough that John Hutchinson's death had been caused by an irritant poison.

An inquest was held at which a Whittlesey shopkeeper, William Hawkins, said that he had sold a quantity of white arsenic to Amy the day before her husband's death. In Amy's defence, several witnesses spoke of John Hutchinson's brutal behaviour to his wife but, as her affair was common knowledge, that was accepted as a just reaction to her infidelity. Not even Hutchinson's certainty that he had not been poisoned helped Amy. Much of what was related in the court was hearsay and, when all was done, only the evidence that Amy had bought arsenic to kill mice was of any real account. It was enough to condemn her.

On Monday 7 November 1748 the inquest jury returned a verdict that 'the said John Hutchinson was wilfully and maliciously murdered by poison'. And there was no doubt about the identity of the person who had administered it. Amy was arrested.

After time spent in Ely Gaol she was tried at the Assizes there. Witnesses were called and evidence was heard to the effect that Amy's marriage had been unhappy. She had been afraid of a brutal husband and she had wanted to be rid of him. The cause of all the trouble,

*Lynn Road, Ely, and the Old Gaol, now a museum.* The author

Thomas Reed, was also mentioned but, although seeming central to all that was alleged to have taken place, he was not required to be in court.

Amy was charged with petty treason, murder by a person in a position of trust or loyalty to someone their better. There were three categories to which petty treason could be applied – a clergyman killing his superior, a servant killing his or her master, or a wife killing her husband. Petty treason carried the death penalty and the method used to carry out the sentence had a horror all its own.

But what could be worse than hanging? Amy, in due course, would find that out.

The trial lasted for less time than it had taken John Hutchinson to die. The jury's verdict, despite Amy's plea of innocence, was that she 'feloniously, traitorously, wilfully and of her malice aforethought did poison, kill and murder against the law of our said Lord the King his Crown and Dignity'.

When the Assizes came, they were a great event, drawing hordes from all around the area. Day to day lives were drab and poor. For the common man there was little of colour and excitement. And then along would come the Assizes and with them street entertainments, music, song, sideshows and stalls, food and drink. Crowds of men, women and children turned up in whatever best clothes they had. It was their holiday, and the best part of it was a hanging day. The highlight was an execution.

And that October in 1749 there were to be two. Along with Amy there was John Vicars, also from Whittlesey and also charged with the murder of his spouse. His case, however, had been more clear cut, literally. He had gone to the shop where his wife was a glover, had made a cut three inches wide and four inches deep in the left side of her throat, and had then waited to be arrested. He said that she had been a whore and that she had to die, even though he had known that he would not want to live without her, the reason why he had just waited to be arrested, bloody blade in hand. He had pleaded guilty and was sentenced to death by hanging.

Amy, too, still proclaiming her innocence, was to die. But not by hanging. She was to be burned at the stake.

Burning at the stake was the method chosen to end the lives of women who had committed high treason, petty treason, or who were witches. It was not a case of letting the punishment fit the crime. They were burned, as one contemporary chronicler stated, 'for the decency due to the sex forbids the exposing and publicly mangling their bodies'. A woman could not be seen dangling from a rope or

*Frost and fog on Palace Green, Ely. This is believed to be where burnings at the stake took place.* The author

being disembowelled by that ogling crowd. Modesty at all times. Light the faggots.

The crowd's reaction to the prospect of a burning can be imagined. Even John Vicars seems to have been impressed. It was usual practice for a woman to be burned at the stake after a man was hung, but Vicars asked if he could go second so that he could see Amy burn. His request was granted.

On a sledge on 7 November Amy was drawn to the site of the stake, believed to have been on the present Palace Green. Her face and hands were tarred and her clothes were daubed with pitch. A short prayer was said, and then the executioner strangled her.

That was the usual procedure, although it was done in various ways. The woman could be seated on a stool or barrel and bound to the stake and a chain or rope put around her neck. As the fire was lit the rope or chain would be tightened and the stool or barrel knocked away. She would be dead before she could feel the flames. It was thought to be a kindness, and her modesty was preserved.

Amy was strangled, the fire was lit, and in half an hour she was ashes, having given her life, at the age of twenty-one, for the love of a man.

And what of that man, Thomas Reed? Had he been worth it? Or had Amy's father's feelings against him been justified?

*Executions took place along Cambridge Road, beyond St Mary's church.* The author

According to a version of events, said to be in Amy's words, which appeared in the *Norwich Mercury* of 9 November 1749, in which she at last confessed her guilt, she damned Thomas Reed. She said that almost as soon as he had returned to Whittlesey and had seen her married he had made threats to her. He had said that if she did not kill her husband he would kill her. He had been the one to suggest poisoning him and he had said that he would kill her if she did not do so. In his thrall, she had administered the poison.

That may or may not have been the truth of the matter. Reed had not been involved in Amy's trial and the case against her had been decided without him. But, tellingly, he never saw her after her arrest, never visited her, abandoned her for a second time, and may even have married someone else before her execution.

Too late for Thomas Conquest to say that he did not like Thomas Reed, but perhaps not for him to say 'I told you so.'

Amy was not alone in being burned at the stake in Ely. Mary Bird had gone before her, also found guilty of poisoning her husband.

She had been imprisoned in Ely Gaol in 1737 but, unlike Amy, she had not been abandoned by her lover. In fact, there had been disquiet in the prison as 'her Gallant so often managed to talk to her' and 'the Gaoler was ordered to strictly forbid his ever being admitted to the Sight of her again'.

It was said to be an unusual event in the country when she was burned at the stake that summer. Both Amy Hutchinson and John Vicars would have been small children then. Perhaps they were brought from Whittlesey by their parents to enjoy the carnival event and 'join the many thousands of spectators whose Curiosity inclined them to the Sight of an execution so uncommon'.

All too soon it would be they who provided the entertainment.

Chapter 2

# The Price of Bread
# 1816

Winston Churchill spoke movingly of the Battle of Britain in 1940 as 'our finest hour' but, over a century earlier, in 1815, the country had enjoyed another hour almost as fine when the French were defeated at the Battle of Waterloo to end the Napoleonic Wars.

Triumph was, however, soon forgotten as Britain was forced into another kind of war – that of living with the peace that followed. Urban and rural discontent among workers spread throughout the country, with East Anglia actively involved.

In and around the Fens unrest took hold in the first months of 1816 and by May had become riot in parts of West Suffolk, Norfolk and Cambridgeshire.

There were many causes for that unrest, especially in areas reliant on farming, but it came down to low wages, high prices and shortage of work. The situation was made worse by the numbers of ex-servicemen returning to their towns and villages, creating a labour surplus at a time when it was a struggle for most families to bring money into their homes, their 'miserable huts', a plight condoned by their superiors as keeping them in their place.

The fear of a French-style revolution by the increasing urban population was intense, and it had spread to the sparsely populated rural areas. But the agricultural labourers of Norfolk and Cambridgeshire were thinking more of bread for their bellies than revolution as unrest stirred in the heartland of the Fens caused, as the Board of Agriculture Report of 1816 said, 'entirely from the want of employment which they are willing to seek but the farmer cannot afford to furnish'.

They had no voice and no rights. In April and early May they expressed their distress in the only way open to them. They broke the new farm machinery, especially the thresher, which was doing the work they sought, and they set fire to ricks, their glow illuminating the night sky far across the flatness of the land.

That agitation may have continued without escalation but for a sudden rise in the price of flour. Bread prices rose, and bread really was the staff of life in every home. The pub and street corner gatherings became demonstrations and then, in mid-May, riot.

Outbursts of 16 May were beyond the fen edges, at Bury St Edmunds and Brandon in Suffolk, and Hockwold, Feltwell and Norwich in Norfolk, and then, early in the morning of Monday 20 May, ferment reached Southery.

There, men assembled for a march on Downham Market to confront magistrates and overseers of the poor at their weekly meeting at *The Crown*. Gathering more rioters as they went, and pressing the reluctant, they marched through Denver and into Downham.

Yeomanry were sent for. Meanwhile, the magistrates were confined to the hostelry in the market place by a mob of 1,500 baying men, and a few militant women, armed with pitchforks, sticks and stones.

On arrival in Downham, some of the rioters had made straight for two bakeries and had taken all the bread they could find. As it was distributed, a deputation of eight men was admitted into *The Crown* to make their demands to the magistrates – for work and two shillings a day. The magistrates agreed. It was a pacification.

The deputation and magistrates then went out into the market place to persuade the rest of the mob to return to their homes, but

*Downham Market Town Square, with* The Crown *located on the right.* The author

The Crown, *Downham Market, as it is now.* The author

they were not in a mood to be persuaded and began to clamour for the release from lock-up of a gang of poachers. Everywhere had its gangs of poachers – meat for free in desperate times – despite the harshness of punishment when caught. They threw stones at the magistrates, forcing them back into *The Crown* to escape through the back door into Paradise Road. The rioters then attacked and ransacked the hostelry, taking food and, of course, beer.

During the afternoon they raided a flour mill, led by twenty-two-year-old Thomas Thody, a married man with two children, and a thirty-two-year-old self-employed single man with his own waggon and team of horses, Daniel Harwood.

The nine women prominent in the riot, the youngest only seventeen, concentrated on the town's bakeries and butchers. Twenty-three-year-old Amelia Lightharness and Hannah Jarvis, a widow of thirty-six, went the whole hog. From one butcher they took 250 pounds of pork.

At about five in the early evening detachments of yeoman cavalry arrived, some coming from Upwell. Dering, one of the magistrates, came out of hiding to go with them to the market place and read the Riot Act. That led to a confrontation but, when arrests began to be made, the crowd at last began to disperse.

It would be back. The next day the Southery crowd was joined by men from Hilgay, some of them again pressed. They marched to

Downham and demanded the release of those arrested the previous day. It is not clear if the poachers were included as they got their way and the men were freed, the magistrates wisely agreeing as they saw that a number of the men were now armed with guns.

With a little more organisation the rioting could have spread far across the Fens. Other places – Soham, Isleham, Whittlesey, March – were ready to take part. As it was, news of the rioters success in getting the magistrates to agree to their demands encouraged only the men of Littleport, a few miles from Southery. They rioted the next day, Wednesday 22 May. Had they not been so hasty, more news might have reached Littleport that, although concessions had been agreed in Downham, the magistrates had no intention of keeping to their agreements. Their only action would be arrests and imprisonments.

As riot began in Littleport, the yeomanry set about making arrests in earnest in Downham Market, including the re-arrest of all those freed by the mob. The time for eating stolen bread was over. The next time that the rioters would be asked to open their mouths would be in their own defence at the Norfolk and Norwich Assizes.

The village of Littleport, close to Ely, was, according to the *Cambridge Chronicle* of the time, 'a dirty place full of mud and mire'.

Surrounded by fenland, the people of Littleport had long opposed any effort to drain it. As far back as 1638, local justices had been alarmed to hear that 600 men were planning a game of football in the streets. Football was a highly suspect activity in the seventeenth century, and with reason. While there was still unease at the prospect of three hundred a side, the men stormed into the surrounding fens and began to break the dykes being constructed as part of Cornelius Vermuyden's drainage scheme.

Nearly two hundred years later little had been gained by the draining that had been carried out. Fishing and fowling had been curtailed but the farmland gained was said to be 'extremely precarious', still liable to be flooded by the Great Ouse.

After hearing of events in Downham, a group of Littleport men met in *The Globe*, supposedly for a club meeting. They were not all farm labourers. Others were suffering from the social and economic conditions of the day and amongst them were a tailor, a bricklayer, a potter, a blacksmith and a publican. One of the riot's leaders, William Beamiss, was a shoemaker.

They streamed from *The Globe* to march to the home of the vicar of St George's, the Reverend John Vachell. He was the obvious number one target. In the close-knit fenland community the blame for much that was taking place was laid at his door. He was an enthusiastic magistrate who revelled in bringing his parishioners to court for the

*Main Street, Littleport, 1903, with* The Globe *on the right.* Cambridgeshire
Collection

*Main Street, Littleport: now a car leaves Globe Lane but* The Globe *itself has
gone.* The author

*St George's, Littleport.* The author

smallest of misdemeanours, and they were treated harshly. As his unpopularity had grown so his congregation had diminished, a sad indictment of his twenty years as vicar to the people of Littleport. They demanded work and bread and asked Vachell to negotiate with employers, and then they went on, roused, to raid several other houses. Riot had begun.

They went back to the vicarage at about eleven that night. Vachell was in bed and came to his front door in his nightshirt, armed with a pistol and wearing his hat. He threatened to shoot any man who entered his home and then he read them the Riot Act, which was in his hat.

The rioters cared nothing for that. Vachell was overpowered and his pistol was taken from him. While his home was ransacked, he fled upstairs to his wife and two daughters, one of whom was seriously ill, and they managed to escape. In their nightclothes, they ran nearly all the way to Ely. Picked up, at last, by a farmer with a horse and trap, they were driven into the town where Vachell reported the riot to the magistrates.

He and his family had a fortunate escape, and would never return to Littleport. While they ran to Ely, their home was torn apart, as were other homes and shops in the village.

The *Cambridge Chronicle* reported the event:

> *A great concourse of people had assembled for the purpose of destruction. Their most furious attack was made on the house of the Revd John Vachell, which began by breaking his windows. They entered the property and broke every article of furniture, with which they pelted the greenhouse, scarcely leaving an unbroken square of glass. They carried off all the family plate, ripped up the feather beds, and scattered the feathers in the street.*

Vachell would later claim damages against the Hundred of Ely under the Riot Act. He received over £708.

The next move for the rioters, with John Denniss to the fore, was to march on Ely to gather support. In the early hours of the morning, as the vicar fled, they took possession of a farm waggon, mounted on it a punt gun used in fen fowling and, armed with whatever weapon had come to hand, they set off.

At the Ely boundary they were met by a magistrate, Reverend William Metcalfe. He tried to stop them, but they would have none of it and went on into Ely, as far as the market place, where they gathered outside the *White Hart Inn*.

Again their demands for work and bread were put to the magistrates, Metcalfe having been joined by Reverend Peploe Ward and Reverend Henry Law. Ely magistrates tended to be clergymen. There was a

*Ely Market Place.* The author

long discussion with, at the end of it, as in Downham Market, an agreement to the rioters demands and a pardon for all who had taken part in the riot. It was the safest way to defuse a nasty situation, but it would amount to nothing.

Satisfied, many rioters made their way back to Littleport, but the hard core stayed in Ely, terrorising inhabitants and attacking homes and shops, until eventually the peace of exhaustion settled over the town.

At that time, with the fear of revolution, Lord Liverpool's government and magistrates everywhere were jittery. Give in to the wants of the common man and where might that lead? They chose to take action against disturbances as they arose rather than to take action against the causes of them. With no professional police force to call on there was, however, no easy way to deal with riot. All that could be done was to call in the army.

And that was what happened at Ely. Word was sent to Bury St Edmunds and Royston for Royal Dragoons to attend, and an appeal for help was sent to Lord Sidmouth, the Home Secretary. He sent the Reverend Sir Henry Bate Dudley, vicar of Willingham and later a canon at Ely, to take charge of the suppression of the riot. He had previous experience of similar events and was known as 'the fighting parson'.

Bate Dudley arrived to find a peaceful Ely with the rioters gone back to Littleport, but that was not to be the end of the affair. On the morning of Friday 24 May, Bate Dudley rode to Littleport with the Dragoons and as soon as they arrived they came under attack. The rioters had barricaded themselves into *The George* public house and were armed.

The *Cambridge Chronicle* reported that, with the arrival of the troops:

> a very severe struggle ensued between them and the rioters, who had secreted themselves in different houses, and were armed with guns, with which they fired many shots at the military, and severely wounded one of the soldiers, but not dangerously. The military then received orders to fire, and the man who had wounded the soldier was instantly shot dead. When this took place the rioters were completely disconcerted, and fled in every direction, but by the perseverance of the military no less than seventy three rioters were taken prisoner.

So keen were the Dragoons, under Major General Sir John Byng, that some of them even swam across the Ouse to make arrests.

And the man shot dead? He was Thomas Sindal, who had been actively involved in the riot at Downham Market, the only man known to have played a part in both riots.

The big guns of the law began to assemble in Ely, making it clear that the government intended the trial and punishment of the Littleport rioters to be a deterrent to others. A Special Assizes for the Isle of Ely was to be held but, for centuries, the Bishops of Ely had had the right to try cases. To do that, the bishop appointed a Chief Justice of the Isle and, in 1816, that was the pompous and ridiculed Edward Christian.

That trial was, however, a Crown matter. It was debatable whether Christian had any right to be there and, with his reputation, he certainly was not wanted. Christian was definite that he must be. He wrote:

*I presume that no person has ever been executed within the Isle from the remotest time where the Chief Justice of the Isle was not present at the trial and who did not sign the Calendar and warrant for his execution.*

Christian, already focussed on execution, did attend as a judge, along with James Burrough and Charles Abbott, but, as William Hobhouse, leader of the Crown prosecution, wrote during the trial, 'giving daily proofs of his Absurdity'.

Christian was renowned, or infamous, for his ineptitude. The elder brother of Fletcher Christian, of mutiny on the *Bounty* notoriety, he was a graduate of St John's, Cambridge, where he had distinguished himself academically. But, called to the bar, he had failed as a circuit judge, so badly that he had become the butt of cruel humour. He had gone back to Cambridge, to Downing, where he had had more success as Professor of Laws. In 1805 he failed to become registrar of the Bedford Level but, soon after, Dr Yorke had made him Chief Justice of the Isle. It was considered a last ditch appointment for an incapable judge. And now he was to take part in the trial of eighty Littleport rioters on a range of serious charges, many carrying the death penalty.

At the start of the trial, Hobhouse dismissed the men's grievances about wages and prices. He suggested that the riots had been organised by outsiders with no connection to Littleport. From the beginning, there was to be an insinuation that the riot had been a conspiracy to damage the government and that agents had been secretly at work in the village inciting the men to riot.

There was never any evidence to support that, only that they had needed work, wages and food. With common sense that would have been understood. There had been various riots and disturbances from time to time through the eighteenth century and they had followed a pattern which should have been familiar. Such riots as took place in rural England were not intended to overthrow authority but were to redress an immediate grievance, usually about the shortage of food or a sudden rise in prices. They were to avoid starvation.

Chief Justice Christian coped satisfactorily on the first day. Hobhouse, who continued to be as sceptical of his abilities as he was of the prisoners pleas of extenuating circumstances, was able to write to the Home Office:

> *I am happy to tell you that the trial before Christian went off very well. His summing up was unexceptionable, except that it was too probing and too pompous.*

Of the resulting convictions he said:

> *I am happy to learn that the Convictions of yesterday have had a very salutary effect on the Minds of the People of Littleport, which were previously very much subdued, and I trust there is no doubt that the general result of the Commission will entirely bring about the Effect which it was the object of the Government to produce.*

It could not have been stated more plainly that the objective of the trial was to set an example, to serve as a deterrent to any other discontent by the lower orders.

He was still concerned about Christian, declaring: 'We must select for the Professor a case of small dimensions, free, as far as human foresight can reach, of difficulty.' But small cases or large, the trial was having the desired effect on Littleport. By the fourth day, Thursday 20 June, the village was said to be panic stricken, awaiting sentences to 'strike terror into the hard part of the inhabitants of this place'.

As the trial neared its end the government was, at last, satisfied. An example had been set and enough had been done to warn the people of the Isle of Ely of the need to obey the law and respect peace and property. Of the eighty appearing in court, twenty-four had been convicted of the most grievous capital offences. Five of them were sentenced to transportation for life, one to transportation for fourteen years, three to seven years transportation and ten to imprisonment for a year in Ely Gaol. The ten to be imprisoned were, instead, sent to the Hulks at Sheerness to await transportation, where clemency was found to be not quite dead. After a few months they were freed 'owing to their good conduct' and each was given 'sufficient money to bear their expenses to his native place'.

The remaining five were considered to be the ring leaders – John Dennis, George Crow, William Beamiss, Isaac Harley and Thomas South. Christian was to put on the black cap for all of them, although it was Mr Justice Abbott who said:

> *Human Justice, however it may be administered, as it is always in this country with mercy, requires that some of you should undergo the full sentence in order that others may be deterred from following the example of your crimes.*

Christian has been criticised as being a 'hanging judge', but he was a man of his time. With death the customary sentence for many crimes, and reforms only beginning to have effect, his shortcoming was, perhaps, that he sometimes let an execution go ahead without resorting to the increasingly expected commutation. He believed himself to be lenient, and said so after sentencing the five rioters to death.

The really damning thing about Christian, and indeed the other two judges, was that he appeared to be totally out of touch with the realities of life for those who came before him. It was plain that, sitting as an arbiter of life and death, he did not appreciate what had caused men to riot in the Isle of Ely. He was keen only to make an example of them, to support the government and prevent the lower classes getting dangerous continental ideas.

He shared Judge Abbott's opinion when he said of the riots:

> *I trust they have arisen from a transient and temporary cause which has made a short progress into the heart of the Isle. The conduct of the rioters cannot be attributed to want or poverty. The prisoners were all robust men in full health, strength and vigour, who were receiving great wages, and any change in the price of provisions could only lessen the superfluity which, I fear, they too frequently wasted in drunkenness.*

The five men were executed in Ely on the following Friday, 28 June, a little over a month after they had marched on Vachell's vicarage, the purpose resounding in Christian's words that their deaths were to be an example to 'I hope for ever extinguish all attempts to excite insurrection and rebellion within this isle.'

They did, but the fact that three judges in Ely had allowed five starving men to go to the gallows reverberated with horror and injustice far beyond the Fens, hastening those much-needed reforms.

*St Mary's, Ely.* The author

In their own locality they were considered to be martyrs to the cause of the underprivileged. As hung felons, they had no right to be buried in consecrated ground, but so strong were feelings in the area that they were interred in a co~~~~~ grave in St Mary's churchyard, Ely, with the vicar's blessing.

*Plaque marking the graves of the five Littleport rioters, executed in 1816, St Mary's, Ely.* The author

There they lie still with, on the church wall close by, a stone slab listing their names and the crimes which led to their execution. And even there the purpose of the government against men who were hungry was marked with the words 'May their awful Fate be a warning to others.'

*Memorial plaque to mark the burial place of the five Littleport rioters, executed in 1816, St Mary's, Littleport.* The author

In August, forty-three Downham Market rioters went before a judge at the Norfolk and Norwich Assizes where nine men and six women were sentenced to death. Most sentences were commuted to hard labour or transportation for life, including those of the pork stealers, Amelia Lightharness and Hannah Jarvis, who were sent to

New South Wales. Only two men, the ringleaders Daniel Harwood and Thomas Thody, faced the hangman.

They were executed before a vast crowd on Castle Hill, Norwich, on 31 August, two months after the Littleport five had dropped into

*St George's and a Harley-Davidson motorcycle. Co-founder of the company was William Sylvester Harley, the son of a Littleport man who emigrated to the United States. Harley was, and still is, a Littleport name. A Harley was one of those hung in 1816.* The author

*Oliver Cromwell's house, now a museum and tourist information centre, next to St Mary's churchard, Ely.* The author

eternity. As in Ely, there was 'the necessity of making severe examples to deter others from similar crimes', but perhaps the executions caused more people to be for the men than against them. The *Norwich Mercury* reported:

> *No malefactors ever expired with greater sympathy from the immense multitude which covered the whole surface of the hill adjoining the place of execution.*

It was just, in 1816, the price of bread.

Chapter 3

# The Death of a Poacher 1823

Sometimes a wife decides that the company her husband is keeping is leading him astray. She tells him so but – well there's no telling him anything. He thinks more of that mate of his than he does of her. And that is what happened to Betsey.

John and Betsey Landen and their child lived at Brandon Creek Bridge in the Norfolk parish of Hilgay, close to the Norfolk-Isle of Ely boundary. Landen, in his twenties, was a farm labourer, but he had recently begun to associate with John Rolfe. Rolfe, a twenty-two-year-old single man, was well-known in the area as a poacher, and Landen was going along. They had already done some chicken stealing together.

Rolfe began to spend a lot of time at the Landen's home. Sometimes he slept all day in their bed and then sat up downstairs at night while the couple and their child slept. Sometimes he was out all night and would come back for breakfast.

Betsey was not happy that he always seemed to be around, sharing her home and having what she knew was a bad influence on her husband. Everyone knew Rolfe for the law-breaker that he was and she wanted her John to have nothing to do with him. But Landen chose to ignore her wishes and to overlook her fears. It was all right.

On the night of Wednesday 29 January 1823, Rolfe was downstairs by the last of the fire. Landen and his wife and child were upstairs in bed. At near midnight – he knew the time because he had Landen's watch in his pocket – Rolfe called up to Landen that it was time for them to go. They had work to do.

Betsey, sensing trouble, tried to persuade him not to go, but he reassured her. Nothing was going to happen to him. She was to go back to sleep and when she woke again it would be morning and he would be home. He would be back before she was awake.

Betsey, still afraid, went downstairs when her husband got up, and she saw that Rolfe had a large bludgeon with him, cut from a chunk of wood. He said that he must take it because if they met anybody on the road who asked them what they were doing out so late he would 'knock him down dead on the spot'. Not what she wanted to hear as she saw them off, her husband carrying a spade, a casting tool.

When Landen left home with Rolfe he had his watch – in Rolfe's pocket – a 'white one' Betsey called it, and £3. He had also put on his new high-lows, made for him by a local Hilgay shoemaker a few weeks before.

High-lows were between a shoe and a boot, reaching just above the ankle. They had rows of hobnails on the sole and perhaps a metal tip to the toes and heels. At that time they were very popular with farm labourers. They were hard wearing, protective and dry. They were the 'must have' for every young worker where Landen lived. Some lads liked to strike sparks with them as they strode along the roads, as did their industrial counterparts in Lancashire with their clogs.

But there would be no sparking that night as he took to the dark, icy road with Rolfe. They were going to a plantation on Jonathan Page's farm in Burnt Fen, about two miles away, towards Littleport, to catch game. They would get a nice little haul, worth good money, and then they would be on their way home.

John Landen was not home by the time that Betsey got up the next morning. He was not back all day, or all the next night. And she saw nothing of Rolfe.

But what could she do? Her husband had gone out poaching, committing a most serious crime. She could say nothing. Do nothing but wait at home. Wait for him to return.

Friday dawned. That morning Jonathan Page's nephew and a friend were to shoot on the farm and the plantation would be a good spot to start. Two beaters went in ahead of them to raise the game birds and they noticed at once that a patch of ground had recently been dug in what had been a boundary ditch between the Isle of Ely and Norfolk. It had been filled in by Page.

They thought immediately that it must be the work of poachers. The 'nightly marauders' were always about. They lifted

*Newspaper extract concerning the inquest on John Landon's body.* Cambridge Chronicle

the earth with a stick carried by one of them, John Staples, and about a foot below the surface they found the body of John Landen – minus his watch, his money and his new high-lows.

When Betsey's husband came home to her it would be in a box.

Three surgeons from Ely, John and Robert Muriel and Robert Stevens, examined the body and presented their findings at an inquest held the next day, Saturday 1 February. Landen had been hit hard on the back of his head, causing a violent contusion and extensive fracture. But the skin had not been broken. The surgeons had removed his scalp and had found, according to Stevens, a hole in the skull he could have 'got a penny piece into'. He had died instantly. One blow had killed him.

Present at the inquest was William Engledow, the Hilgay constable. He had known Landen well. The sight of the body of a friend upset him so much that, although not ordered to do so, he set off at once to arrest John Rolfe. He was certain that he must be the killer. The moment that he heard the inquest jury's verdict he was on his way.

He went to Gravel House, the home of Rolfe's brother, Anthony. Upstairs there, hiding under a bed, he found John Rolfe and said to him: 'John, it is no use to conceal yourself. You must come out.'

As mildly as he had been asked, Rolfe had come out. Well, why wouldn't he? He was an innocent man. Landen had been alive when he had last seen him. He told Engledow that he had left Landen at the gate to his house, but he had seen two men waiting for him on Brandon Creek Bridge, about twenty yards away. They were the ones to ask about Landen's murder.

Engledow was not convinced enough to release Rolfe from custody. About five thirty in the evening he took him to the *Cross Keys* at Fordham. Once there, Rolfe told him more about the two men. He had recognised them as Joseph Pickett and William Nicholls.

Rolfe's father turned up at the *Cross Keys* and he supported his son's story. Pickett, he said, had killed Landen and Nicholls had dug the grave and buried the body. He knew because all four of them had been out poaching. Pickett had killed Landen when he had been stooping forward, either cutting a stick or setting a snare.

Still not convinced, Engledow decided to ask Rolfe about Landen's missing property. What about his new boots, his high-lows?

Rolfe knew what had happened to them. It had been Nicholls. Nicholls had taken them off the body and then had put them in his pockets and had taken them away.

Rolfe's brother Anthony heard him say that. The arrival of a murderer at the *Cross Keys* had been an event. People had arrived to pack the place, Anthony with them. No honour amongst brothers.

He 'coppered' at once. He told Engledow that his brother had been wearing a nice pair of high-lows and had pulled them off as he had heard the constable coming. They were at Gravel House.

Engledow asked Rolfe if they were Landen's, and when he admitted that they were he set off for Gravel House, about a mile away, leaving his prisoner with two people in the crowd that he knew he could trust. He brought the high-lows back to the *Cross Keys* where a Hilgay shoemaker, also in the crowd, said that he was sure they were the ones he had cut for Landen.

So, that was the high-lows accounted for. But what of Landen's watch?

Rolfe said that the watch had not been on the body. It had been in his pocket and he had sold it to a man on Well Bridge on Thursday afternoon. He had got a guinea for it.

Rolfe was searched and was found to have on him eight shillings in silver, a knife, a key and an old purse. The money was what he had left of the guinea. Asked what had become of the money Landen had had with him he said there had been none, except for a sixpence.

Rolfe was detained in custody and was taken to the new bridewell adjoining a new Shire Hall built in Ely. It had been opened in 1822, just a few months before, and the court was so grand that Edward Christian, Chief Justice of the Isle of Ely, had enthused over 'the elegance and beauty of the structure'.

*The Shire Hall, Ely, opened in 1822. It is now a magistrates' court.* The author

*The Old Gaol, about 700 years old, with beyond it the nineteenth-century Shire Hall and other law and order premises, new in 1822.* The author

Rolfe was to appear at the next Isle of Ely Assizes to be held in the Shire Hall at the end of February. There had been some uncertainty about jurisdiction as the body had been found on the county boundary, but it had been decided that the murder had taken place in the Isle. So he was to be tried in the Isle.

As was usual, Edward Christian, after the Grand Jury had been sworn in, made lengthy observations on the heavy case load. But he knew it would be dealt with well. Applying 'flannel', he approved of the high standards of jurisdiction to be found in the Isle and the verdicts returned by such respectable juries.

And then he got on to Rolfe, 'one of the melancholy effects of the game laws'. According to the *Cambridge Chronicle*, Christian 'was led to comment at very great length and read many extracts from his 1817 publication, 'A treatise on the Game Laws', the tendency of which was partially adverse to them.'

But, at last, the trial began with Betsey Landen telling all that she knew of her husband's association with the prisoner. She was said to be in 'a dreadful agony'. Her fears had been more than realised.

She was followed by the three surgeons and Engledow, and then it was the turn of George Creek, a publican at Brandon Creek, near Landen's house. He had been at the *Cross Keys* when Engledow had brought Rolfe in and had been one of those trusted to guard him while the high-lows were fetched and a magistrate brought.

While in charge of Rolfe, Creek had said to him: 'I suppose you murdered him for his money, his watch and shoes?'

Rolfe, he told the court, had replied: 'Yes, and for fear that he should spout.'

They had done that fowl stealing together and Rolfe had become afraid that Landen was getting windy about it, perhaps because Betsey was so against their activities. He might tell someone, implicating him. Several days before he had decided that Landen must be killed. He had known as they set off for Page's plantation that bitter Wednesday night that it was to be then.

Defending the undefendable was never easy. John Hills, a legal representative of Evans and Archer of Ely, tried hard on Rolfe's behalf. He would, he said, tell the court the true version of what had taken place.

It had been self-defence. Rolfe had called Landen to get up and they had gone out together with the casting tool and some snares. They went to the turnpike road and then across some coleseed ground to the plantation. They had had angry words on the road 'respecting an information the deceased wished to lay against one Hubbard' and some more at the spot where Landen had been killed.

Angered, Rolfe had hit Landen with his fist – he had not had a weapon with him – and Landen had hit him with the spade. He had grabbed the spade off him and knocked him down. There had been only one blow, and Landen had said only 'Oh dear!' before he had died. He had then dug the hole, taken Landen's shoes off, covered him with earth, stamped him down and thrown the spade into an old drain.

Rolfe had admitted that what he had told the constable about Pickett and Nicholls had been lies. Engledow had not believed him anyway.

The way in which the constables from several locations and two counties worked together on this case was remarkable. Other constables followed Engledow in giving evidence.

John Bacon, a constable in Ely, had looked for and found Landen's spade, used to kill him, beneath the ice of the drain, leading to Page's farm. Near the drain he had found a bludgeon, believed to be Rolfe's, hidden in the rushes, although Betsey swore that it was not the one that she had seen.

James Weston, a constable in Downham Market, gave evidence about Landen's watch, which he had recovered. His evidence was that William Yallop and a man called Smith had met Rolfe on Well Bridge the day after the murder. Rolfe had told them that he was 'on pad' and had asked Yallop if he wanted to buy a watch. He had said 'not particularly', but he had looked at it and asked Rolfe how much he wanted for it. Rolfe had said thirty shillings. Yallop had offered a sovereign. Rolfe had said: 'Well you shall e'en have it for I am on tramp.' Yallop reminded Rolfe that he had once bought some clothes from him and had looked like ending up at Thetford Assizes for being in possession of stolen property, but Rolfe reassured him. He had bought it from a watchmaker at Brandon two years ago and had paid £3 for it, second-hand. Yallop had bought it and had then sold it to Smith. Weston had recovered it from Smith and had then passed it on to John Bacon. The constables had made secret marks on it so that Rolfe could not deny it was the same watch.

The high-lows also had to be identified as Landen's in court. Engledow said that he knew them from the seventeen hobnails in each one, and Thomas Scott said that he had cut them for Landen. His journeyman, Henry Salmon, said that he had stitched them. He knew his own work.

With the prosecution case finished, Rolfe was asked if he had anything to say in his own defence. He said coolly 'No, nothing.' The jury retired and, almost immediately, returned a verdict of guilty.

Not a whisper was heard in the court, that elegant new court, as Christian proceeded to pass the dreadful sentence of the law, 'which he did in such an impressive manner as produced great effect upon the mind of everyone present, except the wretched prisoner himself, who did not appear to participate in the general feeling.'

Christian, telling Rolfe of the great enormity of his crime, quoted several applicable passages from the Bible, and then said that he must prepare himself to make peace with the Almighty because, on the next Monday, he would be executed. But, all was not lost. Even after his death he might yet be of service to his country as a lasting example of the fate awaiting the murderer. He could have him dissected and anatomised – Cambridge medical school was only a few miles away and was always in need of bodies – but he did not think that would be appropriate in Rolfe's case. He had a better idea for him. He would have his body hung in chains, to keep his bones together when his flesh was decayed, and then he would be suspended between Heaven and Earth, that Heaven which he had so greatly offended and that Earth which he was unworthy to be interred in.

The words of the death sentence were solemnly pronounced. Rolfe showed no feelings. He put his hat on his head and walked away to his fate with a firm step.

Rolfe was executed at Ely on Monday 24 February. Over 5,000 people gathered close to the Cambridge road, beyond St Mary's church, at the usual place of execution. Awaiting death, he confessed

*Vicinity of the Ely gallows, St John's Road.* The author

the crime, said that his sentence was a just one, and warned the crowd against 'bad company and poaching'.

His body was hung for the usual time and then it was 'enclosed in an iron case of chains'. His clothes, including the hood which had covered his head on the drop, and his boots – his own, not Landen's – were covered in pitch to make them weather-resistant.

On the Wednesday, it was taken to Padnal and, besides the Littleport road, it was suspended on a gibbet thirty-four foot high – between Heaven and Earth.

Rolfe had hung and swung there for some time, being of service to his country as lasting proof that crime did not pay, when the Home Secretary, Robert Peel, happened to pass along the Littleport road on his way to visit the Earl of Leicester at his home in Norfolk. He was sickened by the sight of the rotting remains and ordered the body to be taken down.

So, perhaps John Rolfe served his country in a way Christian could never have envisaged.

Robert Peel was to be a reforming Home Secretary, gradually changing for the better the way that crime and criminals were dealt with throughout the land.

## Chapter 4

# There's a Blessed Blaze!
# 1833

Despite the hangings for riot in Norfolk and Cambridgeshire in 1816, rural tension continued and radical ideas began to take hold.

In the winter of 1830 there was unrest on a wide scale as the short-lived Swing Riots swept into East Anglia. Captain Swing was a fictitious hero of the poor fen labourers, taking responsibility for whatever action they took. It was Swing who set fire to farm buildings and stacks or attacked the threshing machines depriving them of work. It was Swing who gave them the nerve to demand employment and better wages.

But, with the coming of spring weather and more seasonal work, the disorder dwindled and Captain Swing went on his way. The cases of incendiarism continued, but they tended then to be the result of a man to man grievance, such as happened at March in December 1833.

In November, nineteen-year-old Robert Brigstock had dug some potatoes for William Vawser, a well-known March farmer. Vawser thought that the job had not been done according to their agreement and he refused to pay Brigstock.

Brigstock, a single man living at home with his parents, was apparently one to stand up for himself and with the nous to do so. He challenged Vawser's decision and, in an effort to get his money, took him to court. But he lost his action, a certain outcome with a labourer against a farmer. He did not get his money and he had to pay the costs.

Leaving the magistrates court, Vawser called him 'a silly young man'. Brigstock's defiant response was that he would make Vawser rue for it and that he would have double his money out of him before the winter was over.

It was a threat that, just three weeks later, Brigstock would carry out.

*Town End, March, early last century, not a beer shop in sight.* Cambridgeshire
Collection

On Saturday 7 December Brigstock, Thomas Story and Thomas
Stapleton met up and did what we would call a 'pub crawl'. Beginning
at midnight they drank in several beer shops and public houses in
March, jollying their way along until they finished up at Edgeley's
beer shop in Town End at two-thirty in the morning.

From Town End, the intoxicated louts careered back towards
the centre of the town, kicking doors and bashing shutters, throwing
stones and breaking windows. Stapleton left the other two then, at
about three o'clock, and they began to make their own way home. By
mischance, their way took them close to Vawser's farm.

Perhaps it was a spur of the moment decision, or it could have been
an idea that had smouldered in Brigstock's mind ever since he had
lost to Vawser in court. As they reached home, he said: 'Now we will
go and set Vawser's stacks on fire.'

Vawser's wheat stack was in his yard, close to farm buildings. Story
was against the idea. 'No. If it were a stubble stack standing by itself I
would not mind it.'

But Brigstock would not be deterred.

About 1830 the lucifer match had been introduced and had proved
invaluable to arsonists across the Fens. But Brigstock had no lucifer.
He went into his house and got a shovelful of glowing embers from his
hearth.

Vawser had gone to bed at nine, having secured his farm for the
night. In the early hours he was awakened by a shout of Fire! He

*March Town Hall, opened in 1900 as a Corn Exchange and Fire Station, too late to save the Vawser's farm. It faces the market place.* The author

charged out of his farmhouse to find his wheat stack on fire and fire already spreading to a stack of haulms, a stable and the outbuildings where his implements were stored.

Story lodged with his sister, Sarah, and her husband, James Hartley. Hartley woke as Story stumbled home sometime after three. He would not say where he had been and went straight to bed.

Brigstock did not go to bed. He was seen sitting on a fence close to the fire, watching the wheat stack burn. Stephen Butcher, a blacksmith and beer shop owner, saw him there as he ran towards Vawser's to let his pigs out and to fight the fire. Brigstock had been in his beer shop a week before and had said, as Vawser passed by, 'Blast him, I will give him a sisler before the winter is over.'

Now, happily sitting on the fence, Brigstock said to him: 'There's a blessed blaze!'

Story seemed to sleep through it all. About seven-thirty the next morning his sister went to his room to call him to breakfast and, shades of Al Jolson, she saw that he was asleep in bed with his hands and face black with soot. She had already found his cap, singed on the top and with burned wheat stalks sticking to it. She knew of the fire, as everyone did. Her husband had been one of those fighting it. Shaking Story awake and brandishing his cap she accused him of being involved in the firing of Vawser's stack. Of course he denied it.

Detection was then in its infancy, but Thomas Elliot, an auctioneer and police officer, excelled himself as a scenes of crime man. He found part of a shovel, with the remains of some turf ashes on it, about a hundred and fifty yards from the fire, and the footmarks of someone running away from the fire. With the skill of Tonto in the *Lone Ranger*, he followed them as they went all the way to the Hartleys' house. In the house he found a pair of Story's shoes to fit the marks exactly.

Deny it as he might, Story was implicated and, soon after, so would Brigstock be. His undoing was the shovel. Emma Shaw, the Brigstock's next-door-neighbour, identified it as the one that she had often seen in Robert Brigstock's house.

Both men were arrested later that Sunday and held in custody in the March lock-up house. The next day, after they had appeared before local magistrates and had been charged with feloniously setting fire to Vawser's property, John Fletcher, the constable guarding them, heard Brigstock say to Story: 'They are listening at the door, don't split.'

Soon after, he set out for Wisbech jail with Story, but he had not gone far when Story said that he wished he had said more to the magistrates, Mr Peyton and Mr Orton. Fletcher said that they could go back, but Story said: 'No, I will tell you and you can tell the magistrates when you get home.' Sensibly, Fletcher had taken him straight back to make his cofession.

The next day when Fletcher was taking Brigstock to prison in Ely, he said: 'I know Story has confessed and I will confess of him.' Ignoring Fletcher's advice to say nothing until he came before the magistrates again, he then gave his version of their rampage back from Town End and on to his home.

Once there, Brigstock said, it had been Story who had said: 'We'll set fire to Vawser's stacks.' He had got the fire, but it had been Story who had made a hole in the wheat stack and had thrown in the shovelful of fire. They had both been frightened by what they had done and had run away.

They both appeared before Mr Sergeant Storks, Chief Justice of the Isle of Ely, at the next Ely Assizes at the end of March 1834.

He opened the Assizes with remarks on the youth of many of the prisoners he was to try and their inability to read and write. Most of them were under twenty-one, 'in a state of entire ignorance,' and were being tried for their lives.

The fire had spread. Brigstock and Story were charged with the firing of a wheat stack, some haulms, a stable, a chaff house and other of Vawser's property. Lengthy evidence was heard from witnesses who knew of Brigstock's loutish nature and his dislike of Vawser. Thomas Elliot told of his detective work. Emma Shaw identified the shovel, and James Hartley told of Story's late homecoming.

Sarah Hartley, devoted to her younger brother, was called upon to tell what she had seen of him the morning after the fire, of the soot on his face and the burned straw on his cap. Her evidence would have been enough to condemn him had he not already made a full confession.

Magistrate Thomas Orton brought a copy of that confession to the court. Of what had happened after Brigstock had got his shovelful of fire Story had said:

*I pulled him back when in the close when the fire fell and he swore at me and called me a fool. He picked it up again and placed it underneath or at the bottom of the stack. It blazed out and I with my cap knocked it out as I thought. It was a wheat stack and the only one in the yard. Brigstock ran away and I stayd trying to put it out. He called several times for me to come away. I stopped till I thought it was put out and then I ran away across the field to Hartley's house. I went the back way and before I got home I saw the fire blazing out. I still went home and went to bed and slept until seven or eight o'clock in the morning. My sister brought my cap up to me and said, 'You were one in the mess, your cap is singed.' I said nonsense and laughed at her. I wiped the dust off my cap and washed my hands. I called at Brigstock's and he was not up. I went into the town and looked at the ruins. I got Brigstock's gun and in two hours he came to me in the field. John Harden was with me at the time.*

> *As soon as he left, Brigstock and I talked the fire over. I told him we were very foolish and the fault was all his. Brigstock said 'I know it now but cannot make up the loss.'*

In court, Story added that Brigstock had told him 'to say nothing about it and it would not be known'. He also identified the shovel, as Emma Shaw had, as Brigstock's.

Story put in a written defence, mostly the same as his confession to Orton except that he pleaded his innocence. He had not been the one to start the fire and he had tried to put it out with his cap.

Several witnesses took the stand to speak well of him. Unlike his friend Brigstock, Story had always been of 'good character'.

Brigstock, the ne'er-do-well, had no defence, his guilt was patent, but his defence counsel was determined to go down fighting. Mr Smith maintained that there was a flaw in the indictment. Under the 7th and 8th of George IV, it was imperative that the crime Brigstock was being tried for should be stated to have been 'unlawfully and maliciously' committed. But it had been stated as 'feloniously, wilfully and maliciously' committed, making it, in his view, invalid. The prosecution did not agree, and neither did the judge. It had been a desperate last stand, and it had failed.

After only a short retirement the jury returned verdicts of guilty with, as both the accused were so young, a recommendation to mercy.

Regardless of that, Storks put on the black cap, the square of black silk to rest on his wig, and said:

> *Prisoners at the bar, after a long and patient inquiry you have been proved guilty of the crime of arson, a crime so enormous in its wickedness and so fearful in its consequences, that not only has the law of the land inflicted upon its perpetrators the severest penalty, but the sense of every man by common assent has agreed that this, of every other crime, deserves the most tremendous punishment. The murderer limits his crime to the death of his victim, and the robber also keeps within a certain extent, but he who sets the torch to property knows not the extent of his destruction, nor is he able to say how many individuals he may injure against whom he has not the slightest feeling of hostility. I am now called upon to steel my heart against the agonizing feeling of a parent, the appeals of anxious friends, or the dictates of mercy, and in administering the law let me warn you against indulging any fallacious hopes of a commutation of punishment. Sacrifice none of the very valuable time which remains to you by clinging to earth nor suffer your thoughts to be distracted from the awful change which awaits*

*you. There are no hopes for you but beyond the grave. There they may be bright and cheering to all who fervently seek to obtain mercy by sincere repentance.*

They were both sentenced to die on the scaffold, to which, it was said, 'they exhibited the most perfect indifference'.

Brigstock and Story were to hang at noon on 24 April, but moves to get them a reprieve began as soon as they were sentenced. The jury had recommended it. Special efforts were made on behalf of Story, who had obviously not wanted to be a part of Brigstock's actions, had done his best to put out the fire and had confessed his guilt. His sister, Sarah, had collapsed on hearing the death sentence and had been helped from court.

Despite her brother having made his confession, Sarah became certain that it was she, giving evidence about the soot and his cap, who had brought him to the scaffold. As the campaign to have him reprieved gathered strength, so Sarah's health dwindled. The date for the execution drew nearer and then, almost at the last, Thomas Story got his reprieve. But, sadly, it came just too late for Sarah. She had 'died of a broken heart, a day or two previous to the respite being received, imagining that her evidence had been the means of convicting her brother'.

There was no reprieve for Brigstock.

By the early 1830s, thanks to long-needed reforms in the justice system, the 220 crimes which carried the death penalty had been reduced to fifteen. With fewer executions, most towns in and around the Fens stopped employing their own hangman. In his place, the London area hangman was often engaged, which is how Robert Brigstock came to be hanged by the executioner for the City of London and Middlesex, William Calcraft, exponent of the ineffective short drop which tended to strangle a prisoner to death instead of instantly breaking his spinal column.

Calcraft was said to be as dispassionate on the scaffold as if he were hanging a dog, and he would sometimes go down into the pit to pull on a prisoner's legs to help him on his way as he continued to struggle against the throttling noose.

It is not recorded whether Brigstock needed his legs pulled as 'an immense concourse of persons at the usual place of execution in Ely,' watched him 'behaving in a becoming manner', undergo the extreme penalty of the law.

A second case of stack burning was heard at the same Assizes on the day after the sentencing of Brigstock.

Young farm servants then were expected to do as they were bidden. They were voiceless and powerless when it came to righting a wrong or settling a grievance. A lucifer or a shovel of fire often spoke for them, or, as in that second case at Ely, a candle in a lantern.

Eighteen-year-old Thomas Thody was charged that on Thursday 2 January 1834 he wilfully and maliciously set fire to the property of his master, Dyson Savage, who farmed in Littleport Fen. Burned in the fire were three oat stacks, four wheat stacks, two hay stacks, a straw stack, straw walls, a calf lodge, a waggon lodge, a barn, stables and pig sties.

A fire more extensive and destructive than the one that Brigstock was to hang for and one of which Savage said: 'Sure as the world I am you set this on fire,' and yet Thody was acquitted.

He too had that priceless commodity possessed by Story, but not by Brigstock – 'a good name'. He was vouched for by a character witness with clout, a 'large farmer' in Denver, who had known him from a child. Storks, in summing up, said that there had been no reason for Thody to start the fire, he had no motives for revenge, and he was not 'of a wanton mind or reckless character'.

With proof against him as strong as that against Brigstock, the jury gave him the benefit of the doubt, and Storks said that they had done right.

## Chapter 5

# Going to Charlotte 1861

I t is sometimes said that money is the root of all evil. It certainly was for Augustus and Charlotte Hilton of the Cambridgeshire village of Parson Drove, a few miles to the west of Wisbech, in March 1861.

The young couple had been married for two years and Charlotte, eight months pregnant, was looking forward to motherhood having lost her first baby. Her future should have been bright, but relations with her husband were not good. He drank more than he should, he was excitable, and he found it hard to control his temper. They argued almost continually. On most occasions about money.

Both Augustus and Charlotte were from families in a prosperous way of business. There was no shortage of money on either side. Thirty-two-year-old Augustus was a farmer and grazier in good circumstances, the son of a wealthy farmer who was deputy lieutenant of Lincolnshire and lived near Parson Drove, just over the border into Lincolnshire. Charlotte, at twenty-three, was said to be one of the best looking women in the area. Small and always neatly dressed, she was amiable and pleasant – but she was far more than that. She was a remarkable woman, the daughter of a remarkable man.

Her father, Charles Barnes, had left Parson Drove in poverty, having borrowed money to see him on his way. About two years later, he had returned, a made man, to buy land, a mill, a bakehouse and a large house – and to repay the loan. He had made his money as a sub-contractor working on the railways then being built.

In 1861, he was still doing so, living at Padley Wood, near Derby. His mill and bakehouse, by Clow Bridge in Parson Drove, he had left in the very capable hands of Charlotte and her fifteen year old brother, Joseph. A younger brother, ten year old George, also helped, sometimes buying corn for the mill.

Living in the well-appointed Mill House with her husband and brothers, Charlotte controlled her father's business interests. She had

*Mill and house, Parsons Drove, 1910.* Cambridgeshire Collection

moved from her own house at Gedney Hill to do that. In her father's absence, she took care of the accounts and all cash transactions. She was very much his right hand, an excellent businesswoman when few had either the ability or the opportunity.

And that was what 'excited the bad passions' of Augustus Hilton.

On Saturday 2 March, Augustus and Charlotte were quarrelling as they left home in the gig at about ten in the morning. They were going to Wisbech market. They quarrelled all the way there, all the time that they were in Wisbech, and all the way home. They reached home at about four-thirty, still arguing.

As soon as they went into the kitchen, the heart of their home, Augustus told Charlotte to get the slate and write down how much money he wanted because she had not given him enough for the wheat he had bought for the mill at Wisbech.

She refused, saying: 'Why did you not ask me at Wisbech? I would have given it to you.' And she went upstairs to take off her coat and hat.

When she came down to tea Augustus was sitting by the fire smoking his pipe and, as he usually did when they argued, drinking a glass of water. He would only drink tea when they were friendly.

He was poured a cup of tea, which he let get cold. Charlotte got down the slate and asked him how much money he had spent and how much he wanted, but he had had a few drinks in Wisbech and was

*Wisbech market today.* The author

beyond being reasonable. He said that she knew how much and she was just to write it down. But the matter was not settled. Neither seemed able to speak or write the sum in question – £17 6d.

Joseph and George and the journeyman miller, Tom Snow, had tea in the kitchen with the squabble about the price of wheat still going on.

Augustus decided then that he wanted his tea, but it was cold. He asked Charlotte to pour him another cup. 'I won't,' she said. 'You have been slandering me all the time I was at Wisbech, and going and coming, and do you think I am coming home to wait on you in this way? No, I won't. I'll die first.'

'So you shall,' Augustus said, and then, 'May I have an egg?'

Charlotte said: 'Yes, you may, and welcome.'

Susannah Tooke, the servant girl, brought Augustus three boiled eggs, which he ate without bread and butter. Joseph playfully pushed him on the head, called him 'Gussy', and poured him another cup of tea before he went back to the mill. Augustus smoked another pipe of tobacco. He didn't drink his tea.

The couple went to sit each side of the fireplace, and still the argument went on.

'You know what you ought to have given me.' Augustus told Charlotte to get the slate.

'If I do you won't tell me what to put down.'

Susannah started to clear the table. Augustus told her to go to the *King William* public house to get him a pint of ale, and she was to take George with her.

'No, George,' Charlotte said. 'Do you stop with me.'

Susannah got a pitcher and put on her coat and went for the ale. Joseph came in and Charlotte asked him to get Tom to put the mare in the gig. Augustus was in such a foul mood she had decided to go and spend the night at her aunt's home nearby.

Joseph tried to dissuade her. 'No, you had better not, it is so windy and rainy.'

But Charlotte was determined. 'Yes, I will. If I stay at home he wont let me have any peace.'

She went to the stable herself to see Tom about the gig.

Susannah hurried for the ale. There was an atmosphere between the Hiltons that she did not like. She wanted to be back with Charlotte. She brought the ale and Augustus was still going on about the money owed to him.

'You know what to put down. Put it down.'

Charlotte had the slate but he would not tell her what to write, so she put the slate away and went exasperatedly upstairs to get ready for the drive to her aunt.

Augustus followed her at once, closing the kitchen door behind him as he went into the passage leading to the stairs. He went up two flights of stairs to Charlotte's room at the front of the house. He closed that door too, and bolted it.

Soon after, there was a scream, and the nightmare for everyone who knew, loved and respected Charlotte Hilton had begun. The nightmare that Joseph Barnes found when he forced his way into Charlotte's room.

'Look you there, Joe,' Augustus said. 'I have done it.'

Augustus had put Charlotte's head under his left arm and had drawn a long pocket knife across her throat from her left to her right ear.

CROWN COURT.

*MONDAY, the 22nd of July,* 1861.

(Before Mr. Justice WIGHTMAN).

**THE PARSON DROVE MURDER.**

ON the evening of Saturday, the 2nd of March last, a most appalling murder was committed on the body of Charlotte Hilton, residing at Parson Drove, in the Isle of Ely, and County of Cambridge, by cutting her throat, at her dwelling-house (as was proved at the coroner's inquest), by her husband, *Augustus Hilton,* a farmer about 30 years of age.

The poor woman was the daughter of Mr. Chas. Barnes, railway contractor and miller, formerly a resident at Parson Drove. Mrs. Hilton had not been married more than two years, and during that time her lot was reported not to have been of the happiest character; for her husband was a man of excitable temper, and quarrels between them were of frequent occurrence. On the day of the murder, it was said they had kept up a quarrel for several hours, and it ceased only with the life of the unfortunate woman. A most painful feature in the whole case is, that the poor woman was, at the time she was murdered, within two or three weeks of her second confinement. Her husband followed her upstairs, and cut her throat, after which he walked deliberately through the house and out on to the road, informing two or three persons of what he had done.

*An account of Charlotte's murder.* Cambridge Independent Press

On the morning of Monday 4 March Augustus came before the Wisbech magistrates charged with the wilful murder of his wife. A fair-complexioned young man, tall and slender, with brown hair and whiskers, he hardly seemed a murderer as he said, as he had when arrested: 'I want to die. I want to go to my wife.'

He would never waver from that.

During the afternoon, an inquest into Charlotte's death was held at the *Swan Inn* in Parson Drove and the people in her life who had been drawn so suddenly and horrifically into its end told, each in their own words, what had taken place.

After the first gruesome duty of the coroner's jury, to go to Mill House to view the murder scene and the body still lying there, the first witness was called.

Susannah Tooke, the Hilton's maid of all work, told her tale of that Saturday and reached the point where Augustus had followed Charlotte upstairs:

*I and the little boy, George, remained in the kitchen. In about a quarter of an hour Tom came to say the mare was harnessed. I told George to tell Charlotte, meaning my mistress, that the mare was ready. Tom said, 'No, don't, she will be down directly.' I heard the chamber door bang and I was afraid that Hilton might be doing something to her and I said to George, 'Do go, he will very likely do something to her.' He would not go. We listened and heard a scream. I ran up and Tom followed me. I tried the door and could not get in. It was fastened inside. I heard my mistress groaning and a scuffling noise on the boards, as if people were struggling together. Tom ran down and called for King and Joseph, and I ran out of the front door and called for Mr Billings. I then went and told Mrs Jealous. I stopped there about ten minutes. While I was there I saw Hilton come out of the yard gate on foot. I went up to him.*

The coroner interrupted Susannah's evidence to ask why Augustus was not at the inquest. He was told by the Parson Drove constable that the Wisbech magistrates had refused to let him attend. He was in the custody of Inspector Stocking of the Isle of Ely Constabulary, who was present, and he was reprimanded for having removed Charlotte's blood-soaked hat and other clothing from the murder scene before the visit by the jury. Susannah then continued:

*Mr Jealous and Mr Billings went up to Hilton as soon as he came out of the gate. One of them said: 'Here is the man.' Hilton said, 'Yes, here I go. I have done it', and he walked on towards the Clow Bridge.*

*I said, 'Yes, and your neck will be stretched.' I said so because I felt sure he had killed her, having heard the scuffling and groaning in the chamber. Mrs Jealous went back with me and I saw some account books on the fire and I took them off.*

Joseph Barnes began by stressing that the milling business and the bakery were his father's and had nothing to do with Augustus. On occasion, Charlotte asked Augustus to buy corn for the mill. She would give him the money to pay for it and he had to account to her. He said that they often argued about money, so often that he took no notice. It was usually trifling.

Of that last fatal argument, he said that Tom Snow had come for him. He had run into the house and upstairs, forcing his way into Charlotte's room:

*I saw Hilton coming from the bed towards the door. I saw blood upon his face quite plainly. My sister was lying across the bottom corner of the bed nearest the window. I saw a large wound in her throat and blood flowing from it.*

He had then run downstairs to call Richard King, the miller, and as they went back to the house together they had met Augustus at the back door. 'I said, "You villain, get out!" King said, "Oh master, what is the matter?" In reply to this Hilton said, "Go upstairs, you'll see." He seemed to be very cool. He put his hands in his pockets and walked out into the yard. I then went upstairs with King. He went and raised my sister up. Dr Sturkey came soon after.'

Joseph, only fifteen, then collapsed in court into 'a state of insensibility which lasted for some time.'

John Thomas Snow, the twenty-year-old journeyman miller who lodged in the Hilton house, made it clear, as had Joseph, that the milling business had been run by Charlotte and her brother. It had nothing to do with Augustus. Augustus, it seems, must have been made to feel that he was very much Mr Charlotte Hilton. He said that he had heard the couple 'jangling' in the kitchen, cutting one another off shortish. Augustus had looked a little wildish and a little worse for drink. He said that Charlotte had been determined to go to her Aunt Brumby's at St Edmund's Common. Coming to him in the stable, she had said that she would drive herself. She was so eager to be away. 'Tom, I'll go. I'll not be with him tonight,' had been her parting words as she had gone indoors to get ready.

He was waiting for Charlotte in the kitchen 'when we heard two or three loud shrieks. We ran to the first landing and heard two or three shrieks again. We went upstairs to the next landing. The girl tried the door of mistress room and we heard only groaning. We both ran downstairs. Ann ran out the front way and I went out the back for Joseph Barnes.' Joseph had sent him for the doctor. After the doctor had gone, Snow had seen 'a great deal of blood about and mistress was then dead'.

The Mill House that Charles Barnes had bought was so substantial that he had divided it and had let half to Daniel Billings, a grocer and draper, for use as a shop. Mrs Bethia Smalls, the wife of a Parson Drove saddler, had been in the shop when she had heard screams from somewhere 'above but not overhead.' Billings had been unconcerned. It was only the Hiltons, quarrelling again. But then Susannah had come to the shop and cried, 'Oh, Mr Billings, do come.'

Mrs Smalls went too and told the inquest jury what she had seen in Charlotte's room:

*On going in I saw Richard King supporting Mrs Hilton on the foot of the bed. Her feet were hanging down on the left side of the bed and she was sitting across the left corner of the bottom of the bed. I asked what was the matter and King said 'Gus has cut her throat.' On removing a handkerchief which King had put on her neck I saw a long wound completely across her throat.*

Charlotte had died soon after, still in her market dress. There was blood everywhere. The room, as Mrs Smalls described it, was deluged and saturated in blood. Preservation of evidence was probably in its early days. Mrs Smalls had never heard of it, at least. She moved everything moveable and took Charlotte's hat from the murder scene, so it was she who should have been reprimanded and not Inspector Stocking.

When Richard King gave evidence, yet again it was stressed that Augustus contributed nothing to the Barnes' house or business. Called upstairs by Joseph, he had seen Charlotte by the light of the candle on her dressing table, her head hanging down off the bed. Tenderly, he had lifted her up and put a handkerchief over her throat. He had held her, her face against his cheek, feeling her gradually dying, until Dr Sturkey had arrived.

The last witness to be heard that day was Hannah Jealous. Her husband's butcher shop was only ten yards from the gate to the mill yard. Susannah had come in crying that Gus had killed Charlotte, and she had gone at once:

*Hilton stood in the kitchen, calmly and deliberately, with his back towards the fireplace. There was a smell of burning. The account books*

*were burning. He said, 'Well, Mrs Jealous, I have done the job.' I
said, 'Oh dear, Mr Hilton, what have you done?' He said, 'I have
done the job and I am willing to be hanged for it.' He had then gone
out to walk to his parents' house in St Edmunds and Mrs Jealous, as
so many others, had gone up to see the carnage in Charlotte's room.*

There were so many witnesses that the inquest had to be completed
on the Friday, so many who would never forget that Saturday evening
in March of 1861.

After 'doing the job' Augustus had gone to his parents' house.
When George Lake, the Parson Drove constable, arrived there he was
sitting by the fire, smoking his pipe and drinking brandy and water.
He was not sober. He had washed the blood from his hands and face
but his clothes were heavily stained.

He asked Lake: 'Is she dead?' Told that she was, he said:'Then I'll
die too. When shall I be hanged? I want to go to my wife.'

His only thought from then on would be to hang and to go to
Charlotte.

His committal was on Tuesday 5 March at the Sessions House
in Wisbech. Mr Ollard of Outwell was to defend him. Brought into
court, Augustus was abstracted. Once or twice during proceedings,
and especially when his father-in-law was giving evidence, he became
agitated and muttering. Charles Barnes, with restraint, said only two
words to him – 'Bad 'un.'

The court was packed, with crowds outside unable to get in.
The Hiltons were well-known and the whole area was roused. All the
witnesses from the coroner's court repeated their depositions. Lake
gave evidence, and Inspector Stocking, who said that, in his cell,
Hilton had asked him, 'When shall I be hanged? I want to die. I want
to go to my wife.' After that, left alone, he had gone on and on calling
out 'to go to his Charlotte.'

As his committal ended he said: 'I wish to go to my Charlotte,
that's all.'

With throngs of people in the road outside the Sessions House,
pressing to catch a glimpse of him, he was hustled into a fly and
whisked away to Cambridge County Gaol.

With crowds again clamouring to get into court, Mr Justice
Wightman took his seat at the Cambridge Summer Assizes. On
Monday 22 July, Augustus was brought before him, indifferent to
court and judge. He was smartly dressed in a black suit with a white
handkerchief in his breast pocket. From the fixed look in his eyes and
the compression of his lips it was clear that his mind was as made up

as it had ever been. He took a firm hold on the rail at the front of the dock and when he was asked how he was pleading his voice was clear and distinct: 'Guilty.'

Wightman explained the finality of that plea and asked Augustus to reconsider. He would not do so.

That, then, ended his trial for murder. Wightman reluctantly, feeling that justice should be seen to be done and had not been in Hilton's case, put on the black cap.

Slowly and solemnly he pronounced the words of the death sentence, deeply affecting everyone present. There was perfect silence and stillness throughout the court until the last word was uttered, and then there came a deep, breathing sound.

Augustus, unmoved, looked round the court. He was taken below without saying a word.

Twenty-eight years after hanging the young farm arsonist, Robert Brigstock, William Calcraft, by then called in the local press the Executioner of England, was to hang Augustus.

The last executions at Cambridge had been those of Elias Lucas and Mary Reader, guilty of poisoning Lucas' wife at Castle Camps, carried out by Calcraft in 1850. Augustus was to be buried next to Lucas in the prison grounds.

The Wisbech press was kind to Calcraft who, since his appointment in 1829, had been much criticised for his callousness and his looks. Of a hanging at Liverpool in 1863, an official at the execution wrote of 'the ghoul Calcraft, with his disreputable grey hair, his disreputable undertaker's suit of black, and a million dirty pinpricks which marked every pore of the skin of his face.' Perhaps both he and his suit had undergone a rapid decline because, hanging Augustus in 1861, the reporter of the *Wisbech Advertiser* found him to be 'by no means a repulsive man'. He was 'dressed in a handsome suit of black' and he had 'bushy white whiskers'. There was no mention of a flower in his buttonhole. A keen gardener, he often wore one of his own roses.

The time appointed for Augustus to go to Charlotte was noon on 10 August. He was never left alone but he seemed not to consider suicide. He was content. Eating and sleeping well, reading, smoking his pipe, and exercising in his own yard.

His father and Ollard worked tirelessly for a reprieve, which failed. Augustus was pleased. He wanted to die, saying: 'I would not live if all Cambridge was given to me.'

As he said his goodbyes to his parents, sister and brother on the Friday afternoon, Calcraft was boarding a train in London, a short noose in his overnight bag. At Cambridge station he got into a fly and was quickly driven to the prison.

As he slept in the governor's house that night he was as much at ease as Augustus who said, as he went to bed, 'I feel very comfortable now and I hope that I shall feel as comfortable tomorrow. I don't see why I should not.'

He slept well. He was still asleep at eight the next morning when the crowds were already gathering at the barricades around the scaffold. They had begun to arrive at five. There would be 20,000 there by noon.

Many of the crowd had been in Cambridge the previous day and had gone to Messrs Bell's to view Augustus' plain coffin with his shroud and cap laid on it.

It was in Bell's yard that the trappings of execution, unused for eleven years, were stored. The same scaffold had been used for all executions at the County Gaol since the first one in 1812, eight years after the prison's opening, and would finally be auctioned for £1 in 1930, sold to a Littleport man.

The barricades to keep the turbulent crowd at bay stretched for a width of fifty feet, twenty-five feet in front of the prison door facing Castle Hill. In that space, a stage was built, about five feet high, and six and a half feet above that was the drop. So high would Augustus be that all of the 20,000 would be able to see him.

At six minutes to twelve the chapel bell began to toll and Calcraft entered the pinioning room to fit the leather harness which, as a cobbler by trade, he had devised to immobilise a prisoner's arms and hands. His legs would be pinioned on the scaffold.

The procession formed. Augustus led the way, nattily dressed in a pepper and salt coat, striped trousers and a dark waistcoat, with Calcraft on one side of him and Reverend Ventris, the chaplain, on his other. Behind came the High Sheriff, the Under Sheriff, the prison governor and several turnkeys. From the gloom of the prison they went out into the heat and sun of an August noon.

Augustus, erect and calm, climbed the seventeen steps to the scaffold unaided and looked over the mass of people as if they were no more than a field of wheat. A few voices called out, 'You're going to Charlotte!'

A prayer, the white hood, the noose, the sliding back of the bolt and the drop fell open with a dull, heavy sound, and Augustus was dead.

The *Cambridge Independent Press* of 17 August 1861, covering the execution, devoted a column to the matter of the abolition of capital punishment. Even then, it was contentious, with reformers and philanthropists working for abolition. Others were as vocal in demanding an end to public executions, and in 1868 they got their way with the passing of the Capital Punishment Within Prisons Act, ending centuries of awful public spectacle. The abolitionists would have a little longer to wait for the last execution of all – 104 years.

*Wisbech Museum.* The author

*River Nene and Brinks, Wisbech.* The author

Chapter 6

# Of the Deepest Dye
# 1861–1863

ohn Garner of Mareham-le-Fen, near Horncastle, Lincoln-shire, was a farmer, beer house proprietor, coal dealer and shopkeeper. In his late forties, he was in a comfortable way of business.

The shop, as usual in a fen village, sold many things, the convenience store of its day. Items of food and drink and household goods made up the greater part of his stock – but not all of it. On a shelf, close to foodstuffs, he had half a hundredweight of arsenic, sold as a vermin killer.

In the early 1860s, he was a man in a household of women. Garner and his wife, Hannah, had lived happily together for a number of years and had been joined in the previous year by his mother, Jemima. And then, in October 1860, Elizabeth Whittaker moved into the Garner home, and with her came change. She was to work in the house and wait in the shop, and nothing between Garner and his wife and mother was to be the same.

Soon after Whittaker's arrival Garner's attitude to his wife altered. Hannah suspected that her husband and the new girl were on too familiar terms and she let it be known that she was determined to get rid of her as soon as possible. The response that she got from Garner was physical violence. On more than one occasion she had to run out into the street to escape his assault, aided and abetted by Whittaker.

Hannah was close to Ann Shepherd who had previously worked for the Garners until her marriage in 1858. Garner had then put Ann and her husband in charge of his beer house, which adjoined the shop.

About eleven o'clock on one night in early March 1861, when Ann was in bed, she was awakened by knocking on her door. Opening her window and looking down, she saw Jemima Garner who said that Hannah had jumped out of her bedroom window. Hurriedly, she part-dressed herself and went down to find John Garner, angry at what his wife had done but not concerned for her welfare. Ann found Hannah along the street in her nightdress. She said that Garner had been swearing and hitting her and she had been forced to save herself from his violence.

Only days later, on the following Saturday, Hannah was taken seriously ill. Ann found her, upstairs, extremely sick, purging and very thirsty. Jemima was also sick. Ann gave Hannah cold water, which she drank 'greedily', and then she went into the shop and got the arrowroot drawer from just above the shelf where the arsenic was kept. She cooked some of the arrowroot to make a food thought to be good for stomach complaints. It seemed to do Hannah good. She went in regularly over the next few days to make arrowroot for her with Whittaker taking no interest at all. She totally ignored her mistress.

Hannah had continued to purge for more than a week when Ann, preparing the arrowroot, ate some of the food herself. It made her violently sick. She was in bed for two days, managing to visit Hannah just to tell her of her sickness before going back to her bed again. She was so ill that for a time she lost the use of her limbs. She never fully recovered.

On 28 March, while Ann was struggling to cope with her own illness, Hannah died.

Garner's malice then centred on his mother. He was seen to kick and beat her and, on one occasion, he and Whittaker turned her out of the house and told her to go to the Union, the workhouse. Jemima said to a friend that she wished she had never broken up her own house and gone to live with her son, adding, 'I am sadly in the road for them, and I am afraid of them.'

She had good reason to be afraid. On 20 December, two weeks after saying that, she was dead.

It seemed a natural death of an old lady, and was dealt with as such. But, as so often happens in small, close communities, rumours began. Tales of cruelty against Jemima by Garner and his new wife – yes, he had wasted no time in marrying

LINCOLNSHIRE.—*Alleged Arsenical Poisonings.*— On Friday evening week an inquiry was concluded at Revesby, a few miles from Horncastle, Lincolnshire, into the circumstances attending the death of an elderly woman, named Jemima Garner. The inquest, which has been several times adjourned, took place at the Red Lion Inn, and was conducted by Mr. Walter Clegg, coroner for the district. The deceased died many months since, and sinister rumours having been prevalent as to the manner in which she came to her end, her remains were exhumed about six weeks ago, and a post-mortem examination made by Mr. Bolton, of Horncastle, and Mr. George, of Revesby. The result was that the stomach, intestines, heart, liver, and a portion of the spine, were sent in sealed jars to Professor Taylor, who reported that he had discovered a large quantity of arsenic. John Garner, of Mareham-le-Fen, son of the deceased woman, and Elizabeth Whittaker, who had lived with the parties as servant, and who since the death of the poor old woman had married the son, were apprehended by Superintendent Thoresby, of the Lincolnshire constabulary, on a charge of wilful murder. The evidence adduced at the various sittings of the coroner's jury showed that the prisoners had behaved cruelly to deceased. Thus it was stated that Garner had been seen to kick and beat his mother, and on one occasion he and Whittaker put her out of the house in which they lived together, and told her that she might go to the Union. About a fortnight before her death the deceased remarked to a person named Welldon, that she wished she had never gone to her son's house and broken up her own home, adding, "I am sadly in the road for them, and I am afraid of them." The investigation resulted in a verdict of wilful murder against both prisoners, and they were committed for trial at the next assizes at Lincoln.

*Allegation of arsenical poisoning and inquest.* Cambridge Chronicle

Whittaker – were spread abroad. And there was the matter of the sickness and death of his first wife, Hannah.

It was not long before, walking into the Garners' shop, came Superintendent Thoresby of the Lincolnshire Constabulary.

The bodies of both women were exhumed and post-mortems were carried out by the eminent pathologist Professor Taylor, of Guy's Hospital, London. At the inquest into the death of Hannah, held in January 1862, he reported his findings. Arsenic. Everywhere. It was in her liver, heart, intestines, muscles, ligaments and spine. The presence of arsenic saturating the liver, he said, made it probable that she had ingested a large dose shortly before her death.

The post-mortem on Jemima proved as conclusive. She too had been poisoned with arsenic.

John and Elizabeth Garner stood trial for the wilful murder of both women at Lincoln Assizes on Wednesday 18 March 1863, appearing before Mr Justice Willes in a court 'crammed to a degree only to be imagined. Every available space where it was possible for a human being to sit or stand was occupied.' They pleaded not guilty.

The charge relating to Jemima came first before the jury. Mr Stephen, for the prosecution, began with a one and a half hour speech relating Garner's cruelty to his mother and the finding of arsenic in her body. He made it clear that there was no doubt that Jemima Garner had been poisoned. The question to be answered in court was who had done the poisoning. Both prisoners had had easy access to arsenic and the opportunity to administer it.

*The Garners charged with murder.* Cambridge Chronicle

## THE LINCOLNSHIRE POISONINGS.

On Friday week, at Horncastle Police Court, John and Elizabeth Garner were charged with the wilful murder of Hannah Garner, the wife of the male prisoner, who died on March 27, 1861. From particulars with which we furnished our readers a fortnight ago, it will be remembered that the prisoners had already been committed for trial on the coroner's warrant, also that the body of the deceased had been exhumed, with the sanction of the Home Secretary, in consequence of suspicions which had arisen, and that the result was that a quantity of arsenic was found in the remains, on their being analysed. The principal witness examined before the magistrates on Friday was Ann Shepherd, who went to live in the service of John Garner about fourteen years ago. She left there to be married seven years since. Mrs. Garner and Shepherd, according to the evidence of Garner's daughter, were extremely fond of each other, and this will account for the great attention the latter paid to the deceased in her last illness. When Shepherd first went to live with Garner he and his wife were pious people, and lived very comfortably together. A few years afterwards, however, he sometimes quarrelled with his wife. About three years ago Shepherd and her husband were placed by John Garner in a beer-house of his, which adjoined the shop in which he lived, and was under the same roof. About October, 1860, Whittaker, the female prisoner, whom Garner married a few months ago, went to live with Garner as servant. She was to do the general work of the house, and to wait in the shop. Soon after this the conduct of Garner to his wife changed for the worse. The wife suspected that her husband and Whittaker were on too familiar terms, and frequently expressed a determination to get rid of her as soon as possible. A few weeks before Mrs. Garner died, Shepherd, while in bed, heard some one knocking at her door. This was about eleven o'clock at night. She opened her chamber window, and heard either Whittaker or the grandmother (Jemima Garner, who died subsequently) say that Mrs. Garner had jumped out of her chamber window. She accordingly partially dressed herself and went down stairs. Garner was in the house, and was very angry at what his wife had done. Shepherd went out of doors to look for Mrs. Garner, and eventually discovered her on the road in her nightdress. She stated that her husband had been swearing at and beating her, and that she had jumped out of the window to escape from him. At this time Whittaker was in the habit of abusing her mistress very much. On another occasion, after this, Mrs. Garner had to rush from the house to save herself from her husband's violence. On the Saturday or Saturday week following, Mrs. Garner was taken seriously ill, and Shepherd was sent for by her. On going up-stairs she found Mrs. Garner violently purged and sick, and she complained of excessive thirst. The grandmother was also very sick. At the request of Mrs. Garner, Shepherd gave her some cold water, and then went into the shop and fetched the drawer containing arrowroot and made her some food. This drawer was placed just over the shelf where about half a hundredweight of arsenic was kept. Shepherd tasted the food and then gave it to Mrs. Garner; it apparently did her good. Mrs. Garner continued in this state for some days, Shepherd occasionally waiting upon her, and cooking arrowroot for her. No medical man was sent for, and Whittaker treated her mistress during the whole time with the greatest neglect. Mrs. Garner continued to be violently purged and sick up to the Monday week after she was first seized. On this day Shepherd again prepared the arrowroot, and ate a large portion of it herself. She was afterwards violently sick and ill, and was confined to her bed for two days. On Wednesday she again went to see Mrs. Garner, and informed her of her illness, and she then prepared some more arrowroot for her, but did not herself partake of it. Shepherd afterwards became worse, and was confined to her bed, and she had never been well since. For a long time she had no use in any of her limbs.

Witnesses were called, and almost all their evidence was of the bad treatment of both prisoners to Jemima, but especially of John Garner. He had been seen to ill treat his mother and she had been turned out of the house several times.

It was then proved that large quantities of arsenic were kept in John Garner's premises. He sold arsenic to his customers, just as he sold food. The prosecution case concluded with Professor Taylor telling of finding arsenic in all the old lady's organs, and he produced in court parts of her intestines, stomach, liver and heart as proof.

The defence did not question that. It was accepted. She had been poisoned. When Mr Sergeant O'Brien addressed the jury for two hours on the second day of the trial what he dwelt on was the lack of evidence on how she had been poisoned and who had done the poisoning. In what was to become a masterly performance, he suggested that Garner had arsenic 'loosely distributed in various parts of the house'. Arsenic was kept near to food. The thrust of his argument was that it was very possible, and probable, that arsenic might have accidentally become mixed with the household's food. It was, O'Brien believed, more than possible that death had been caused by the 'culpable negligence of the prisoners' in their care of the poison and not by any wilful design on Jemima Garner's life. She had died from arsenical poisoning, but it had been the result of an accident, or even of suicide. If either had been the cause then both the prisoners must be acquitted. If the arsenic had become mixed with food through culpable negligence then they were guilty of manslaughter. Only if it was absolutely certain that one or both of them had given the poison deliberately would it be the jury's duty, both to God and man, to return a verdict of wilful murder.

A superb defence which Willes was reluctantly compelled to reprise in his summing up, reinforcing its assertions. After a retirement of only ten minutes the jury returned, and O'Brien had done his job. They returned a verdict of guilty of manslaughter not murder.

The court was stunned, as was Willes. 'Then you find the prisoners guilty of culpable negligence in the management of the drug which got mixed with the food and was administered to the old lady?'

'Yes, my Lord,' the foreman replied.

. 'And so I am to conclude that you believe the direct cause of the old lady's death was in consequence of culpable negligence?'

'Yes, my Lord.'

The jury's verdict had appalled Willes and the entire court, with the exception of the Garners and O'Brien. Consulting prosecution and defence at that point, Willes decided that there would be no point in going ahead with the Garners' trial for the murder of Hannah as it could not result in a verdict more favourable to them. That was agreed and Willes proceeded, letting his feelings in the matter come to the fore as he led up to sentencing them:

> *I am dealing now with persons who have properly and justly been placed on their trial for wilful murder by the administration of arsenic, against whom proofs of very great weight existed, which proofs it was necessary should be considered by a jury. The jury have, however, not considered them sufficient to satisfy them that you actually put the arsenic into the food of the old woman with a design to kill her. But, at the same time, they have found you guilty of causing her death by gross and culpable negligence in the management and care of a poisonous drug which you both knew to be in the neighbourhood of food with which it was likely to become mixed, that food being sold by you to people in the neighbourhood and administered to the inmates of the house.*
>
> *It is a strange and extraordinary fact in this case – and it was one of the facts which required and which received the grave attention of the jury – that you yourselves did not suffer from that which caused the sufferings of so many. I am, therefore, dealing with a case in which not only has death been caused by your gross and culpable negligence in dealing with a deadly drug, but I am dealing with the case of persons who were so grossly negligent as to others and not as to themselves.*

*High Street, Lincoln, with today's Courts of Law adjacent.* The author

*The Magistrates' Court, Lincoln.* The author

*I am dealing, therefore, with an exceedingly bad case, though not one in which the jury have felt they could pronounce a verdict of wilful murder, and I should not be faithful to my trust if I did not say, and say it not only by my lips in stating the reasons of my sentence, but express it in the sentence itself, that in the verdict of manslaughter*

*The County Court, Lincoln.* The author

*which has been pronounced is one of the deepest dye. I have stated my reason why I think the gravity of your offence and the protection of the public, which is the end of all law, requires that I should pass upon you the weightiest sentence that the law allows, that you respectively be kept in penal servitude for the rest of your natural lives.*

St Andrew's Church, Ramsey Road, Whittlesey. The author

*Late seventeenth century Buttercross, Market Place, Whittlesey.* The author

The harshness of the sentence showed plainly that Willes thought that, courtesy of a good defence and a merciful jury, the Garners had got away with murder. John Garner tried to say something, but no words came. Elizabeth Garner's eyes filled with tears as she followed her husband from the dock.

Chapter 7

# What Green Did to Brown
# 1863

In March 1863, John Green and William George Smedley worked as maltsters at Thomas Whyle's maltings in Whittlesey market place.

On the evening of Wednesday 11 March they worked until eight o'clock when they locked up and went to the *George and Star* public house next to the maltings, where a dance was under way, perhaps an ongoing celebration of the wedding of the Prince of Wales and Princess Alexandra of Denmark the previous day. The place was packed. Not a seat to be had. The landlord said that there were some spare benches in the storeroom. He gave Green the key and told him to help himself.

He did help himself, and to more than benches. He found a large container of gin, filled a bucket from it and then hid it behind some

*Whittlesey town sign.* The author

*Market Place and* George Hotel, *Whittlesey.* The author

planks of wood in the pub yard. He went back to the tap room to tell Smedley and they decided to take the bucket to the Malthouse.

Smedley, as Whyle's head maltster, had the keys to the yard and the kiln room, and he kept watch while Green smuggled the bucket in. The gin was then poured into a stone jar. After that, they sat in the warmth from the furnace, smoking, pouring gin from the jar into a quart pitcher, and drinking.

To cover the theft, Green said that the bucket must be taken back where he had found it. Smedley agreed, saying, as they left the kiln room, 'We won't lock this door as we may be returning again, but we will lock the big gates.'

The dance was still going on. Just before midnight Green went to the tap room for some beer, and there was thirty-six year old Elizabeth Brown, a regular at the *George and Star*. They knew each other, but then, Betty knew a lot of men. She was what was called 'a loose character'. She was with her friend, Ann Macdonald, and Green chatted them up. He bought them a drink and then he suggested that they all go into the maltings. It was warm in there, cosy, and there was drink.

Green, as under maltster, did not have a key to the Malthouse. They went outside, where he hoped to find Smedley. He was the one with the key. They stood about on the pavement. It was, by then, one o'clock in the morning and it had become chilly. There was no sign of Smedley.

*St Mary's with its glorious spire, close to the Market Place.* The author

Betty was cold, tipsy and impatient. 'Can we get into the maltings?'

Green assured her. Smedley or no, they would get in. 'Yes. I have a bottle of gin there.'

'Then let's go.'

Ann decided to go home. Betty and Green went off together, Green holding a bottle of beer. They walked, as Green later said, 'Around by

Mr Waddelow's, by the church wall, through the little gate and into the yard of the *George and Star*.' There, they had climbed over the wall into the maltings' yard.

Once in the warmth of the kiln room Betty was happy, drawing on her long clay pipe and swigging gin. They settled comfortably and then, after about half an hour, Green wanted sex. Betty said no.

In an instant everything changed. Green flew at once into a violent rage and grabbed her by the throat, strangling her. He then dragged her to the floor, punching and kicking her, completely out of control. Only when he had gone too far did he stop to think.

Betty Brown was almost dead. He thought that he had killed her. What was he to do? He was where he was not supposed to be. He was a twenty-four year old married man with a family and, in a drunken temper, he had killed a prostitute. There was only one thing that he could do – get rid of the body. No body, no worry.

And the perfect solution was there beside him. The furnace. He would put Betty in the furnace and burn her. But, as soon as he tried, there was a snag. Her body would not go through the furnace door. Using the iron furnace rake, he tried to break her limbs so that she would fit in, but it was not easy and he gave that up. Anyway, he had another idea. He would burn her where she lay on the floor. He took some sacks from a settle and put them round her before he set fire to them with a shovelful of hot cinders. He then sat down on a block by the furnace to watch her burn.

After about an hour he got up, had some more gin and poked the sacks to hasten the burning. And then, despite the horror of his situation, the warmth and the gin got the better of him and he fell asleep sitting on his block.

When he awoke, the kiln room was full of a thick, vile smoke. With difficulty, he found his way out through the coke store and into the yard. He climbed over the wall and was soon on his way home – home to his wife and three children, the youngest a baby only ten months old.

At about six o'clock Smedley went to work as usual, but nothing was to be usual about it. He saw smoke coming from the kiln room. He rushed in and found a door leading from a passage to the kiln was on fire, as was a settle along the wall. He wrenched the door off its hinges and put out the flames with a few buckets of water. Only then did he notice the charred body lying on the floor, head towards the kiln and feet towards the furnace. Smoke was coming from its chest.

Smedley suspected at once that his workmate was responsible, but he was the man with the keys to the maltings, he had let Green in there, and now he looked like being implicated in some horrific death unless he was smart. So, he tidied up. He swept the room round Betty and disposed of the ashes, and he threw away the jar and the pitcher. Only when he had done that did he run out into the market place and raise the alarm.

The police, led by Superintendent Smith, were soon on the scene. Dr Robert Henry Crisp was called to examine the body and his findings began a major murder inquiry.

The next person to turn up at the Malthouse was John Green. There was no sign of the police. Smedley said to him: 'Here's a job happened. I cleared the pitcher and things out of the window.'

'Do they know who it is?' Green asked.

The top part of the body had been burned beyond recognition. 'No, I don't think they do yet.'

But Smedley was wrong, just as Green had been in thinking that the police were no longer about. As he went out into the yard, there was Superintendent Smith.

'What time did you leave the maltings, Green?' he asked.

Green bumbled, 'Sir, sir, about eight o'clock, sir.'

'What time did you go home?'

'I went and had a pint of beer with my mate and was home in bed by eleven o'clock.'

'Did you see anything of Elizabeth Brown last night?'

Despite the charring of the body Smith had discovered its identity. A purse with her house key in it had been beside her and recognised as hers. Green's answer to that question would be crucial. Ann Macdonald had already told her tale to the police, and a witness had seen a drunken Betty getting over the wall into the maltings. With her had been Green.

'I did see her in the *George and Star* tap room,' Green admitted. 'But I never saw her afterwards.'

Smith had his answer. 'John Green, I apprehend you on a charge of causing the death of Elizabeth Brown who was found dead and burning in the maltings this morning.'

'Oh, pray don't, sir, pray don't,' Green wailed.

With Green on remand, an inquest into Betty's death was held at the *Angel Inn*, Whittlesey, at which Ann Macdonald told what she knew. But John Cunnington's evidence was just as damning. Only minutes before Smedley had discovered the fire at the maltings he and his brother-in-law had met Green near the market place, on his way home. He had his head down but they had known that it was him. Shortly afterwards, Smedley had raised the alarm and had said to them, 'Poor Jack Green is burnt to death.'

Cunnington said:

*I, amongst others, hastened to the spot, when my brother-in-law said, 'It is not Green, for we have just met him going home.' Smedley then sent me to call Green, which I did. I tried his door, which was locked. His wife came to the bedroom window. I said I wanted her husband and Green then came to the window in his nightclothes. I told him he was wanted at the Malthouse. He said, 'I'll be there directly.'*

Smedley was questioned about the kiln room door lock which, according to him, was difficult and may not have locked when he turned the key. Fingers crossed, that would keep him in the clear.

The inquest was adjourned and resumed after a post-mortem on Betty's body by Dr Crisp and Dr Edward Clapham, a house surgeon at Peterborough Infirmary. First, Dr Crisp told the jury of his examination of Betty in the maltings.

*I went to Mr Whyle's malt kiln at half past six o'clock. I went into the kiln furnace room. The first thing I saw was some burning sacks on the settle. I then saw the body lying on the floor of the furnace room, at the further end with the head resting against the door. The door was burning and there was smoke coming from the lap and chest of the body and from the noise made on my throwing water on the chest I have no doubt the viscera were then burning.*

*As the place was dark, I had the body removed to the pump room which was lighted. I got a door to put the body on. When I was assisting to move the body, I took hold of the left forearm. It gave way, as if broken. After the body had been removed I saw an oblique fracture of the bone. The lower end of the bone protruded and was not covered with flesh. The bone was discoloured by smoke but was not charred nor blackened by the fire.*

Very oddly, he had found that a piece of that fractured forearm bone was missing. He had looked, but had not found it.

He had then got on to the post-mortem and, as gruesome detail followed gruesome detail, everyone in court needed to have an iron-clad stomach. Betty had died, Drs Crisp and Clapham decided, from involuntary asphyxia. She had been strangled. And some weapon had been used to break the arm. The bone in question was produced in court, bloodstained and scorched and 'still exuding a strong smell of roasting'.

But, as if that had not been shock enough, there was more to come. Crisp, revealing the most awful conclusion of all, said that the burning of Betty's body had preceded death. She had been burned alive.

Green was found guilty of wilful murder and was to stand trial at Cambridge Winter Assizes at the end of December.

With him would be Smedley. The police had always had doubts about him but the decider that he had been involved had been his work with the broom when he had 'most unaccountably sought to remove all traces which would lead to the detection of the murderer'. Among the ashes that he had disposed of had been the missing piece of Betty's forearm.

The pair pleaded not guilty, and that was the verdict on Smedley. He got away with it. He was acquitted and left the court a free man. Green had no hope of doing so.

Faced by 'a chain of evidence which in its connecting links all but saw the deed committed', there could be no escape for him. As the judge remarked, Green's crime was 'one almost without parallel since the time of the first murder'.

He was sentenced to death and his appointment with Mr Calcraft, the hangman, was fixed for nine o'clock on the morning of Saturday 2 January 1864 at the Cambridge County Gaol, where, in the summer of 1861, Calcraft had sent Augustus Hilton on his way to meet Charlotte, the wife he had killed.

Green began the last week of his life indifferent to his fate and to his religious duties. He did not much care about his hereafter, but more could not have ben expected from 'a man possessed of but very meagre intellectual faculties, and those uncultivated.' He had had little education and could hardly read.

Coming so soon after Hilton's execution, it was inevitable that comparisons should be made in the local press. Most of them related to the two women concerned. Charlotte had been 'of comely appearance and engaging manners' and had been well-spoken of by everyone. But poor Betty 'was not one with whom people would have so much sympathy as with a virtuous and affectionate wife. Still the fact that Elizabeth Brown was a woman of abandoned character, a common prostitute living by her unholy gains, in no way extenuates the offence of her murderer.'

John Green could not have been the ideal as a husband and father, but his wife took her future widowhood badly when she visited him in jail in the days before his execution, taking the three children with her, the baby held in her arms. His parents, three brothers and three sisters also visited him and they talked, but not of the murder and not of his end.

*An end to the Cambridgeshire County Gaol, was where Green was kept during World War One. Here, in 1930, it awaits demolition. The present Shire Hall was built on the site.* Cambridgeshire Collection

But an end there was for Green, said to be tall, fine and strong as he went to the drop dressed in his best white smock with a red handkerchief at his neck, corduroys and sturdy hobnailed boots.

It was a cold, raw morning in the New Year of 1864. Long before nine o'clock the crowd began to gather. And what a crowd it was. From dawn came 'streams of dirty, sullen looking men and still dirtier, wretched-looking women' with, amongst them, 'troops of boisterous rustics'. A murderous under maltster from Whittlesey with a bucket of stolen gin drew them there. 'No gladiator, butchered to make a Roman holiday, ever attracted a more motley, gasping, anxious crowd than did the execution of John Green for murder.'

William Calcraft did his job at nine o'clock. A man of 'not particularly refined conversational powers', he remarked, as he came down the steps from the scaffold, 'There, you couldn't have finished him off much quicker!'

Green was cut down at ten o'clock and, at four, he was buried in the prison grounds, next to Augustus Hilton.

Chapter 8

# Sleep Tight
# 1840s–1860s

ttempts had been made to drain the Fens but in the early decades of the nineteenth century isolated marshy areas remained. There, many of the people, living far from a doctor, unable to afford one, or believing in self-cure remedies, suffered from damp induced conditions such as neuralgia, rheumatism and a malarial-type illness – fen ague.

The Fens were the unhealthiest place in England and one of the poorest. Life was mean and joyless and depression was a common complaint. But the fen dwellers had one friend to turn to, cheaper than alcohol. In most gardens white poppies grew – *papaver somniferum* – the opium poppy.

Poppy-head tea had long been made as a remedy for ague and a soother for babies. The seeds of the unripe heads, boiled in sweetened water, contained morphine and codeine. If gin was added the drink was a tonic. A bonus was the blessed euphoria that might be induced, easing the wretchedness of daily life.

It all seemed as innocent as sugar, and then, from about the 1830s, opium became big business. Commercialisation came and large-scale import, mainly from Turkey, and opium eating became common amongst all classes everywhere in the country. That opium began to be brought into the Fens in large quantities and found a ready and increasing market for its many forms – grains, pills, pieces, syrups, lumps, powders, drops and draughts – all available from every shop and market stall. Virtually every person, man, woman, child or baby, consumed opiates in some sort of preparation. They became a way of life and, all too often, a way of death. What once had been mother's 'little bit of elevation' became an addiction, necessary in most homes.

Most homes, in that way, housed a potential killer. Overdoses, accidental or otherwise, were commonplace, with death rates in the 1850s higher in the Fens than anywhere else in the country, as high in the small agricultural town of Spalding as in many a squalid northern city. The death rate for babies under one year in Wisbech in the 1860s was above that of industrial Sheffield.

Opiates settled crying babies, and some believed that they were beneficial and would 'bring a baby on', but how easily the settling could be made permanent through an overdose. Accidental, of course. It was understood that unwanted children died. That illegitimate babies usually died. That one twin baby would die, if not both. To be born in the Fens in the nineteenth century was a chancy business.

In 1850, when a *Morning Chronicle* reporter investigated opium use in the Fens, a St Ives doctor said to him: 'It is my firm belief that hundreds of children are killed in this district by the quantities of opium which are administered to them.'

Belief was one thing, proof was another. What was clear, however, in many of the cases which reached the criminal courts, was the role played by the women of fenland. They were the ones who bought, handled and administered the drug, who advised others on its use and took that advice, who lent and borrowed it as easily as a spread of butter.

**CAMBRIDGESHIRE ASSIZES.**

We stated in our last that the commission of assize for this county was opened on the previous afternoon. After leaving the County Courts the learned Judges (the Lord Chief Baron Pollock and Mr. Justice Coltman) proceeded to Trinity College Lodge, where they received as usual visits from the Vice-Chancellor, Heads of Houses, and Proctors of the university, as well as the Mayor and Corporation of the borough. Shortly before four o'clock their Lordships attended divine service at Great St. Mary's church, where a sermon was preached by the Rev. Mr. Rickards, of Sidney Sussex college, from I. King's, ch. 21, v. 2, 3.

**SATURDAY.**

At ten o'clock this morning the learned Judges proceeded to the Courts, the Lord Chief Baron taking his seat for the Nisi Prius business, and Mr. Justice Coltman presiding in the Crown Court, before whom the following gentlemen were sworn on the

**GRAND JURY.**

Hon. ALGERNON HERBERT, Foreman.

R. G. Townley, Esq., M.P. | S. Newton, Jun, Esq.
J. S. Tharp, Esq. | B. H. Wortham, Esq.
W. H. Cheere, Esq. | W. Booth, Esq.
W. P. Hamond, Esq. | C. F. Foster, Esq.
Thos. Mortlock, Esq. | R. D. Fyson, Esq.
T. S. Fryer, Esq. | S. Dunn, Esq.
Eben. Foster, Esq. | G. Fisher, Esq.
John Dobede, Esq. | T. Thrusher, Esq.
Wm. Layton, Esq. | C. Finch, Esq.
Edw. Hicks, Esq. | G. Hall, Esq.

The usual proclamation against vice and immorality having been read, his LORDSHIP proceeded to address the Grand Jury. He said that he was very sorry to see by the calendar before him, that there were several cases of a very serious nature. There were two of the prisoners charged with murder, by the coroner's inquests one, named Crabb, of Littleport, was accused of the wilful murder of his wife; but there was not, according to the depositions, any person who was at all able to give a precise account of the transaction.

Babies and children who died, having been given an opiate by the female carer in their life, usually their mother, were often described, if the case reached court, as ailing, weak, sickly, never well, sick from birth, restive, always crying or a cross baby. That justified the giving of the opiate. When death came it was always a surprise to the mother and quite inexplicable. In most cases, it was very difficult to prove deliberate overdosing, and juries returned their verdicts accordingly. It was all that they could do as women throughout the fens and into the surrounding area perhaps got away with murder.

Two cases, both involving a mother who had killed her son with an overdose of laudanum, were tried at the same Cambridgeshire Assizes in Cambridge in

*Two cases of child death from laudanum at the same Cambridgeshire Assizes, March 1848.*
Cambridge Chronicle

*High Street, March.* The author

March 1848. Mary Rumbelow of Littleport admitted giving her son laudanum. It was her habit to do so and she had given him the usual dose. She was charged with manslaughter. Sarah Scarborough, living in March, denied having given her son laudanum, although it could be proved that she had. She made several untrue statements before she reached court, charged with murder.

Before either woman came before a jury, Mr Justice Coltman, deeply concerned, said that he found it remarkable that laudanum should be so freely sold and so carelessly administered. But it would be twenty years and many deaths later before anything approaching the control of opium reached the Fens and, even then, it would still be available and its use would continue.

Sarah Scarborough was twenty-six, single, and an opium addict working as a domestic cleaner to keep herself and her son, William. Leaving work one evening she asked her employer if she could have an empty bottle as she wanted to go to Dawbarn's and buy a penny-worth of castor oil. She was given the bottle, but two assistants in Dawbarn's drapers and druggists, and a customer, would swear that she bought two pennyworth of laudanum on the evening of Wednesday 14 July 1847.

The next morning William, had been found 'in the sleep that knows no waking'. She had called her next-door neighbour, farmer's wife Sarah Moss, and then a succession of friends and relatives to try to decide if he was alive or dead. Three hours went by before a doctor was called to decide the matter for them.

Dr Henry Wright, surprised at the comfort and cleanliness of the boy's bed, decided that death had been due to congestion of the brain, possibly produced by an overdose of laudanum, a diagnosis which would be confirmed by another March doctor and by Dr Letherby of the London Hospital. On post-mortem of the boy's stomach he found that a large dose of opium had been taken.

Despite everyone liking Sarah and considering her a devoted mother, that finding branded her a liar. But she had already lied. She had said, after her arrest, that she had not been in Dawbarn's for over six weeks and had not bought or administered laudanum.

As she stood trial, she denied poisoning William and had not known what was the matter with him when he would not awaken. She said: 'I was a good mother to my child and always worked hard for it.'

Throughout, William was mostly referred to as 'it', and his identity was questioned as much as the manner of his death, thanks to an effort by Sarah's defence counsel, Mr Naylor, to use that to have the trial stopped. He submitted that the child, being illegitimate, could have no name except by reputation. He had been called William Scarborough in the indictment, but it was known that he was sometimes called 'Coley', after his father, and sometimes 'Sarah Scarborough's child'.

The judge would have none of it. There was evidence enough that the boy had been William Scarborough. But failure on that issue only sent Naylor on to another on Sarah's behalf. She had lied. So what? She may have lied about buying the laudanum to hide her own addiction and because of the shame that she might think would attach to her of negligently leaving the laudanum so that the child might get it and she being the cause, though innocently, of the death of her child. The jury might believe that the child had poisoned itself. If, however, it really believed that Sarah had given the poison to the child – then she had not intended to do it. It had been an accident. She had been tired. The house had been dark. How easily she might have given him an overdose.

Naylor's appeal was persuasive and one to touch the hearts of all the members of the jury. And it worked. Sarah was found not guilty of William's murder. She was acquitted and free to go home to March, an outcome which caused the editor of the *Cambridge Independent Press* to write:

*We cannot reconcile the prisoner's conduct with entire innocence as the evidence fully bore out the crime of manslaughter and we fear that the merciful view of the case taken by the jury was misplaced.*

In the other case of opium poisoning before the same court, twenty-two-year-old Mary Rumbelow, a married woman, was indicted with the manslaughter of her baby, John, by giving him sixty drops of laudanum, which she admitted.

John was a cross baby and never well and she usually gave him laudanum or Godfrey's Cordial at night to help him to sleep. Godfrey's Cordial was widely used as a baby settler, 'a dark brown horrible mess' prepared by local druggists to their own recipe of an opiate mixed with treacle, syrup, liquorice or aniseed.

The day before John died, in October 1847, Mary went to Cheesewright's grocers in Littleport. She had intended to buy Godfrey's, but she had bought a pennyworth of laudanum instead. She gave him a third of a teaspoonful that night, and the next morning she had found him dead, killed by an overdose that she knew should not have happened. She was in the habit of giving John laudanum and she knew what a safe dose was.

When she appeared in court, so did Robert Cheesewright who had sold her the laudanum. Unlike Dawbarn in March, who prepared his own laudanum on his premises, he bought his from 'a reliable source in London'. The only explanation he could give was that he had received a batch of unusually high strength. That was accepted by the jury, although no other of Cheesewright's many regular customers for laudanum had been affected. Only John Rumbelow.

*Main Street, Littleport.* The author

The verdict was that Mary had not intended to harm John. The manslaughter charge was dropped and she, like Sarah, was acquitted, with the judge's approval. He said that there had really never been any sort of foundation for the charge.

Babies and small children continued to die through the 1850s and into the 1860s from being given opium, laudanum, poppy-head tea, syrup of poppies or Godfrey's Cordial, their mothers, if brought to court, usually being found not guilty of giving their children 'those dangerous and insidious poisons'.

The women of the fens killed their babies for a variety of reasons, pressured by their personal circumstances and made accepting of the use of opium by custom or their own addiction.

There were many cases typical of the times and of life in fen communities, such as that of the sickly, illegitimate fourteen-month-old who, in the harvest time of 1853, was put into a clothes basket and taken into the field where his mother was gleaning, having been given a piece of opium so that he would sleep while she worked. Joshua died as he was carried home. The young mother and all her family were opium eaters and she chewed opium as she was questioned at the inquest. She was reprimanded, but that was all. The baby, it was decided, had died of natural causes.

Adults addicted to opium died too.

As a one-month-old ailing baby, Eliza Waters, died from being accidently fed an overdose of syrup of poppies in Prickwillow in the New Year of 1863, Mariann Dawson, in her mid-twenties and the wife of a Ramsey labourer, also died. Shown at the inquest into her death,

*High Street, Ramsey, at the end of Victoria's reign.* Cambridgeshire Collection

under coroner Thomas James at the *Spread Eagle* in Ramsey, was the way in which fen women formed their own community, bonded together by a belief in and a reliance on the taking of opiates.

Mariann had lung disease. Two days before her death, on the Friday afternoon, she went to her neighbour, Mary White, for a bit of opium to ease her in getting her breath. Mary White said: 'I live close to her and I am in the habit of taking opium. I said I had not any.'

She next saw Mariann at seven the following evening, in the *Seven Stars*, kept by her daughter. She was very ill and could hardly stand. She staggered in and asked Mary White if she had got any opium. She thought that she was feeling so ill because she had not had her laudanum and she always made it a rule to have it between four and five in the afternoon. She said: 'I felt in my pockets and gave her a bit about as big as a tare.' Of that, Mary White's daughter told the court:

> *I knew she was in the habit of taking laudanum. She had had a piece of opium in my house as big as a tare. She asked mother for it and mother found a small bit which I divided and gave her. My mother will occasionally lend a neighbour a bit of opium. She said nothing gave her so much ease.*

As matter-of-factly as the other women, Mariann's mother-in-law told the jury:

> *I believe she was in a decline. She had an illness some time since and used to raise blood. She was seldom well long together and complained of shortness of breath. She was in the habit of taking laudanum, a pennyworth a week.*

She had also known that she had taken some opium on that Saturday. She had asked her how much she had taken and she had said a piece about as big as a pea.

Mariann had spent that Saturday reeling about her neighbourhood, as though she had no life in her or was very sleepy, but she had at last gone home to her husband and little boy. When her in-laws had called later that night they had found her extremely ill with her head down between a table and a chair and her eyes half-closed. She had died in the early hours of Sunday morning. An end to the perigrinations, the quest for opium, of a dying woman.

Despite the prevalence of opium taking, Mariann's doctor, Dr Bates, claimed that he had not known that she took it. Perhaps not, but it could have been assumed that a woman with a debilitating lung disease would. Almost everyone in the Fens, from the newborn to the senile, took opium.

The medical profession, often not consulted, tended to turn a blind eye to the habit. Taken with care, there was no proof that it shortened life, only that it affected the mind. One Soham doctor believed that it was the cause of the 'feeble-minded and idiotic people frequently met with in the fens'.

Dr Bates had been called to Mariann at midnight, 'who, I was given to understand, had been taking a poisonous quantity of opium'. She had been moribund and there had been nothing that he could do for her. In his opinion, the dose of opium that she had taken had accelerated her death.

Concern at the high death rates in the Fens, especially of babies, eventually led to action four years after Mariann's death. In 1868 the Pharmacy Act was introduced to control the availability of opium, but it was still to be had from druggists.

Its use continued into the twentieth century, with pharmacies still dispensing opiates. But less. There was change, change for the better. There were far fewer deaths and fewer young addicts. The habit of opium eating grew old along with the fenlanders of the drug's heyday. They now bought their little bit of opium as a treat after they had collected their old age pension and, here and there, just a few white poppies continued to grow.

Where's the harm in a drop of poppy-head tea!

## Chapter 9

# Unholy Matrimony
# 1914

In August 1914, war was appalling the nation and the local papers were full of atrocities, injuries and deaths in the aftermath of fighting at Mons. They wrote of the Cambridgeshire men wounded there and the Red Cross train bringing them back to Cambridge.

They featured, too, the plight of Belgian refugees and their arrival in Britain, an event which was to give Agatha Christie the idea of making one refugee a private detective – Hercule Poirot.

In School Place, Peterborough, however, the war was of another kind – between a husband and wife, John Francis and Sarah Ann Eayrs. The marriage of the fifty-three-year-olds was a bitter one. They fought constantly and their near neighbours missed none of it.

It was a time when working class people often lived in close proximity in dwellings small and cramped. There was little diversion in their lives apart from going to the pub and keeping an eye on what the neighbours were doing.

The Eayrs could be relied on to entertain. Their fights went beyond the verbal. There was violent behaviour on both sides, which was worst on Saturdays when they both might have had a drink to put a spark to their ever-smouldering intolerance of each other.

And it happened on Saturday 22 August.

Machine-hand Harry George Masters, across the way from the Eayrs at 11 School Place, looked out of his front window and there were the Eayrs, fighting on the ground in front of their house, number four. He went to his door and Sarah broke free and walked off down the street. Eayrs went into his house to come out again shortly after carrying a basket. He went in the same direction as his wife, towards the adjoining Albert Place.

A few minutes later, just after six, Sarah came back and went indoors to appear at an upstairs window, looking towards Albert Place. When Eayrs came back at six-forty, his wife was still at the window.

*Albert Place street sign, Peterborough.* The author

She laughed at him and Masters heard him say: 'All right you ——.
You will get all you want before the morning.'

Eayrs went up the passageway and tried his side door. Sarah had
locked it so he went into the back yard and returned with a hammer to

*School Place has gone, but Albert Place remains as a commercial area between
Bourges Boulevard and a car park.* The author

*The Eayrs' home area as it is today with the Rivergate Centre, ASDA store, car park and busy dual carriageway.* The author

force it open. As soon as he went indoors, Masters heard the smash of glass, and then he saw Sarah running up the back yard pursued by Eayrs.

Masters watched the warring Eayrs until nearly eight o'clock, as did other neighbours. It was a free show.

*Bourges Boulevard as it passes Albert Place.* The author

Earlier in the evening, Elizabeth Griffin, the wife of a gardener who had lived at number five for two years and had witnessed the breaking down of the Eayrs marriage, had heard a crying Sarah say to Eayrs: 'If you give me my money I can go and do my shopping.' His reply had been: 'I will give you shopping you ——. I will do you in before the night is out.' Later, she too saw her at the window, and saw her put her tongue out at Eayrs.

Henry Carter, a moulder living in Albert Place, stopped to speak to Eayrs as he went along School Place. Sarah was still at the window, which was slightly open, and she shouted down, 'Don't you believe what the liar says. I caught you with a woman.'

Carter was shocked to hear Eayrs say: 'Get in you old ——. I will black your face again for you if you don't.'

'Don't do a thing like that,' he pleaded. Sarah had still been 'nagging' at the window when he had gone on his way.

But Sarah Eayrs had at least one friend. Jennie Rodgers. She had lived next door to the Eayrs, at 2 School Place, until a week before and knew all about the threats that Eayrs made to his wife, usually that he would do her in. She had only moved a few yards away, to a house in Albert Place, and Sarah visited her there at about five on that Saturday. She had gone home to the street fight and when she had freed herself from that she had gone back to Jennie Rodgers. She had been crying then but she stayed only a few minutes before going home again and up to her window.

Just over three hours later, at about nine-thirty, Jennie went into her back bedroom and she was certain that she heard Sarah call her name, twice. She told her husband, William, and asked him to go to number four, just to make sure that Sarah was all right.

Going up the passageway beside number four, William Rodgers heard moanings coming from the back yard. Eayrs was in the yard, beneath a window, with his face and shirt covered in blood and his throat cut.

He hurried at once to the market place and brought back Police Constable Pooley. They found Eayrs lying on the ground, semi-conscious. Close to an outbuilding, lying face downwards in its own blood, was the body of Sarah Ann Eayrs. Her throat had been cut.

Police surgeon Dr R W Jolly was soon there and after examining Eayrs, finding blood on his hands and clothing and a bloody knife in his pocket, sent him to Peterborough Infirmary. His throat wound, unlike Sarah's, was not serious.

Inside the house, the police found a blood-covered razor on the window ledge over the kitchen sink. There was a bloodstained flannel and blood on the mirror over the sink. On a table was the razor case and a poker. There was a broken glass sugar basin in the living room and, on the table, a blood-covered jacket and waistcoat, marks on them probably caused by an axe found at the foot of the stairs.

Eayrs soon recovered from the self-inflicted cut to his throat and, when charged with the wilful murder of Sarah and his own attempted suicide, he was well enough to growl, 'I know nowt about it.'

Later, he elaborated that to, 'I do not recollect anything about it except that a sugar basin hit me in the eye.'

From Dr Jolly's post-mortem, it was determined that Sarah's death was due to a haemorrhage caused by her neck wound. Six inches long, from the bottom of her right ear, it had severed main arteries and veins. It would have taken considerable force to inflict it.

After lengthy committal proceedings before magistrates early in September, it was decided that Eayrs was guilty of Sarah's murder and would stand trial at Northampton. But, before that, there was the inquest. Eayrs was brought from prison in Northampton, although he would not say a word. All the neighbours from School Place and Albert Place, who had already told their stories at the committal, told them again. Deputy coroner, Mr W B Buckle advised the jury to decide if there was enough evidence to indicate Eayrs as the person 'on whom suspicion might reasonably and properly be fixed', and they quickly decided that there was.

Northampton Autumn Assizes were opened at County Hall in mid-October before Mr Justice Avery. Eayrs already had two guilty decisions against him but, defended by Mr Bernard Campion of Messrs Wyman and Abbott, Peterborough, he stood his ground. When charged, he said, 'I know nothing at all about it', and he pleaded not guilty.

For a third time the School Place witnesses were called upon. With them was a photographer who had taken photographs of the murder scene, and Sarah Eayrs' brother, a Peterborough milkman, who had identified the body.

When Eayrs went into the witness box, he said that the quarrel had started on the Friday night 'over a ha'penny'. On the Saturday evening she picked up a sugar basin and hit him in the eye with it. Dr Jolly confirmed that there had been a scar over his right eye. But that was the extent of what Eayrs could tell the court. 'I can't tell anything more after that because I don't know anything.' She had thrown the sugar basin and bolted out of the side door and he had not seen her after that.

The next thing he remembered was waking up in the Infirmary. He had then said to the police officers at his bedside: 'Has my old woman been up to see me?' Told no, he had then said: 'It's jolly funny she has not.'

Cross-examined, Eayrs admitted saying that he would like to do something to his wife, but he had not done something and he had no idea how her throat came to be cut.

Campion said that, despite talk of doing her in because of the miserable life he had with her, it had just been how his class of person expressed anger. It had not been a real threat. The only question to be answered in court was whether he was guilty of murder or manslaughter. No doubt with the sugar basin in mind, he said that if a person who had been struck immediately turned and assaulted his assailant in such a way as to cause death it might be manslaughter. But if a person who had received a blow went in search of a weapon and then pursued and killed his assailant it was murder. In a round about sort of way, Campion was trying to convince the jury that, despite the two verdicts of murder against him, Eayrs had really committed manslaughter.

A waste of time and effort. After only ten minutes the jury found Eayrs guilty of wilful murder. Stunned, hardly seeming to comprehend, he stood in a silent court to hear the death sentence passed.

To the last words, 'May the Lord have mercy on your soul', the High Sheriff's chaplain added 'Amen', and then Eayrs, still stunned, was taken below by a warder.

## Chapter 10

# A Rum Old Boy
# 1929

For twenty-five years, until 1929, seventy-one-year-old Wallace Benton had worked a smallholding in Tilney St Lawrence, near Kings Lynn, an area of farmers and market gardeners.

Well known among his neighbours, Benton had grown mainly fruit, and he had also had success with gladioli. But, in recent years, he had allowed his land to lose heart. It had begun to grow old along with him until it no longer paid its way. The farm had become run down and dilapidated and had slipped into debt as he became more and more a cantankerous old boy, garrulous, short-sighted and as deaf as his gatepost.

By 1925 he was 'in low water'. In 1926, in an effort to keep his smallholding going, he had mortgaged it. But that had been no help at all. He had been unable to pay the interest and all that he had done was delay the inevitable for three years. His mortgage company took possession of his smallholding on 17 January 1929. He was to leave the land and house, shared with his wife Ruth, by the end of the month.

The farm was soon let to a nearby farmer, Thomas Williamson. With Benton's agreement, he took over the land and its buildings at once, but Benton and his wife were given a bit more time to move out of the house. That time was stretched by Benton. They had, after all, been in there for a quarter of a century.

In mid-March they were still there, although some of their possessions had been moved to the gig house of a neighbouring farmer, Robert Judd, and the decision was made to prepare an ejectment warrant. The Bailiff of the County Court at King's Lynn, Albert Haigh, was to carry out the warrant, and Benton knew that. He and Haigh chanced to meet in Lynn market and they had heated words about it. An excited Benton said that he would shoot anyone who tried to turn his wife out of her home.

*Tuesday market, King's Lynn.* The author

Forty-five-year-old Williamson was ready to make a go of the old Benton place. He thrived on hard graft. He had worked his way up from being a farm foreman to taking on his own place and he was keen to make a start. He began to cultivate Benton's land, and he put his horse in the stable. When the Bailiff served his warrant the house

*County Court, on the first floor of 12 King Street, King's Lynn.* The author

would be his too and he would be glad to have Benton leave. The old boy made him nervous the way he went about with his gun, on cock.

At about six o'clock on the evening of Thursday 21 March, the day before Haigh was to arrive at the house, Williamson was mucking out his horse in the stable. A few minutes later he was dead. By six-thirty

Benton was at the home of PC Daw, about three-quarters of a mile away. There had been an accident at his place, he said. When asked what he meant Benton said: 'A bad gun accident. That man who comes on the premises is shot.'

Daw got on his bike. He found the stable door at the Benton place open. Inside the stable was the body of Williamson, feet towards the door. His cap was just beyond his head, as were the rear hooves of the horse tethered there. An old single-barrelled shotgun was lying on the left side of the body, resting on the shoulder, and its muzzle was about four inches from a large wound on the left side of the head. Williamson's hand was touching the barrel. He had, it seemed, shot himself.

Benton joined Daw in the stable and said that Williamson had accused his wife of stealing some chaff for her pony. That, like the Bentons, was still in residence, and Williamson wanted it out.

'We had a few words and he knocked me down,' Benton said. 'I went indoors and got the gun to show him. I knew it was loaded. He caught hold of the barrel and it caught my sleeve and went off.'

He showed Daw the tear in his sleeve. He next said that he had a bandaged finger and the bandage had caught the trigger. And then he said that Williamson had shot himself. He rambled on so much that Daw became unsure what he had said, or if he had.

And that was just the start of a criminal investigation and trial that Benton was to befuddle at every turn.

Daw was quickly joined in the stable by more police, and by Dr J L Forrest from nearby Terrington St John. Despite it seeming that Williamson's wound was self-inflicted, Forrest soon decided that it was not.

Asked, 'What about this job?' by Inspector Hazlewood of the Terrington St Clement police, Benton replied, 'It was his own fault. What he got he deserved.'

Benton was arrested and charged with Williamson's murder.

On Saturday afternoon an inquest was held by the coroner for the Duchy of Lancaster, W J Barton, at the *Buck Inn*. Benton, who at that stage had no representative, was brought in by a police officer. He looked around the court and said that he was surprised that his wife was not there.

Although mentioned at several points through the inquest and subsequent trial Ruth Benton was never to appear. She remained, like Arthur Daley's wife in the television series *Minder*, 'her indoors'.

Barton, who would need to be a patient man, asked Benton, 'Would you like to give evidence?'

'Evidence?' he responded. 'More than a dozen times I have told them about it.'

'Do you want to give evidence or not?'

'I can tell you what I have already told the police.'

'Very well. I must caution you what you say will be taken down in writing.'

'That's what they told me before. You can take it down in writing if you take it down right.'

'Are you a smallholder?'

'No, I am not. I have been dispossessed. I am nothing at all.'

'Well now, tell the jury and me what you know about this affair.'

'I know how the job occurred.'

'You do know how the job occurred, do you?'

'Yes, of course I do. I was there, wasn't I?'

'Well, what can you say?'

'A good deal, but I am handicapped. I cannot hear what you are saying. People get a bit stingy with folks who are deaf. Everyone does.'

'Well, I will try not to.'

'There was a quarrel because he let the pony out of the stable. He shoved me and I fell over the cart shafts.'

'Had you got your gun?'

'They took my gun away.'

'Yes, I know, but when you had your quarrel had you got your gun with you?'

'No, no, no. Not then. He accused my wife of stealing some chaff.'

Barton then produced the gun and asked Benton if it was his.

'Yes. Let me have it and I will show you how it was done.'

Benton was given the gun. He took his coat off and then walked up the room with the cocked gun under his arm and showed how he had confronted Williamson. He had known that Williamson was afraid of the way he went about with his gun.

'Had you your gun with you when you went to the stable?'

'He was talking to me. When he saw this gun he dropped his fork and made a dive for it. He got hold of the gun and dragged at it and it went off.'

When asked to sign his statement as the truth Benton refused, which Barton said was just as well.

He and Daw had both endured Benton's verbal wanderings. The judge at his trial had that pleasure to come, leading him to pay tribute to the skill of the court shorthand writer in producing what appeared to be a connected story.

In summing up, the coroner said that Benton was 'evidently a curious man'. Curious or not, the jury found him guilty of murder.

By the time that he appeared before Sir Travers Humphreys at Norwich Assizes on Thursday 16 June Benton had representation. It was the task of Gerald Dodson, engaged by the King's Lynn firm of Sadler and Lemmon, to defend him. Leading the prosecution was Sir Henry Curtis-Bennett KC.

When asked to plead, Benton indicated that he was deaf. The officer with him in the dock shouted, 'Are you guilty or not guilty?'

'Not guilty,' Benton replied.

'I understand your client is deaf,' Judge Humphreys said to Dodson. 'Have you satisfied yourself that he understands the nature of the charge?'

'Yes. I have, by the generosity of the solicitor instructing me, Mr Gallienne Lemmon, had a speaking tube provided, and with the assistance of that I have found no great difficulty in making the accused man understand.'

Aware of what had taken place at the inquest, when Benton had waffled his way through proceedings to everyone's confusion, Humphreys must have been relieved that he had signed a document stating that he was content to leave his defence in Dodson's hands. But, despite that, the case was to be so memorable to Sir Travers, who had previously been involved in the trials of Oscar Wilde and the murderer Hawley Harvey Crippen, that he was to include R v. Benton in his *Book of Trials*, published in 1953. He admits there that he had difficulty in preserving the dignity of a court engaged in trying a capital offence when 'circumstances combined to create an atmosphere of pantomime'.

Albert Haigh, called to give evidence, told the court of Benton being allowed to stay on in his house for the time being while he looked for other accommodation. But it had dragged on and Benton had known that his days were numbered. In a very roused state, he had called to see Haigh on 5 March and had asked him when he was going to turn him and his wife out of the house. He said that he did not care about himself but if anybody touched his wife he would shoot them. Later that month had come the meeting in Lynn market place. Benton had wanted to know when he was going to the house with a warrant. It would take more than the bailiff on his own to turn him out, he said.

Haigh planned to execute the warrant the next day, 22 March, the day after the shooting. He said:

*Benton did not know from me when I was going to execute the warrant, but he may have got to know. I have had some funny customers when I have been bailiff. Some of them use language which is explosive and unparliamentary. I was impressed by Benton's remarks because I knew the man. I am quite serious in saying it had an effect on me. In this case, I made arrangements with the police to execute the warrant.*

Judd gave evidence that he had not known Benton had stored his gun at his place, and one of his workmen said that on the afternoon of the shooting he had seen him in their yard with a long, brown paper parcel, narrow at one end. Collecting his gun from Judd's, Benton had said it was a window blind.

All was well so far. But, with Daw, the befuddlement began again, although Sir Travers prepared the jury for what was to come by explaining that Benton had made a number of conflicting statements, mixing up the events of the day with others which had taken place many months earlier. He had also contradicted almost everything that he had already said.

Daw was clear about going to the stable and finding the body. The problem was Benton's statement. Exactly what had he said – or not said?

Daw said Benton's words were, 'He accused my wife of stealing some chaff for her pony. We had a few words and he knocked me down. I went indoors and got the gun . . .'

Sir Travers interrupted, 'Did you give this in evidence at the police court? It does not seem to have been taken down. Go on.'

'. . . to show him. He caught hold of my sleeve and it went off.'

'Is that what you have written?'

'Yes.'

'Is there anything about "catching my sleeve"?'

'Not in my notes, my Lord. It was a rambling statement.'

'Tell me anything you can remember. Did he say anything about it catching his sleeve?'

'Afterwards he made a rambling statement and said "it caught my sleeve." He showed me a tear in his sleeve. He said one of his fingers was injured. It was bandaged and he said the bandage caught the trigger.'

Dodson then had a go at Daw. 'You said the prisoner said "We had a scuffle". Did he say that?'

'No.'

'If you saw your signed deposition would you alter your statement?'

'He did not say that.'

'Do you mean that you say you did not say that before the magistrates?'

'I did not say it, but I signed it.'

'You have given another different version this morning. You said he said "We had a few words." Did he say that?'

'Yes, in his ramblings. It was a rambling statement.'

'And about the gun catching his sleeve. Did you forget to tell that to the magistrates?'

He had. PC Daw must have been very glad to leave the witness box. All that rambling.

Walter Allen and his wife had been working their allotment close to Benton's place on the evening of the murder and had heard a shot. He gave evidence that they had looked across and had seen Benton with a gun under his arm walking up and down in front of the stable and then going inside.

After Dr Forrest had told the jury that Williamson's wound could not have been self-inflicted, a gun expert, Mr Churchill, took the stand to corroborate that. He had tested Benton's weapon, which occasionally misfired, and scotched the 'bad gun accident' claim. He had found that the gun would not have discharged easily – with a sleeve or a bandage. The standard pull was four pounds and a light one three. The strength of the pull on Benton's trigger was five and a half pounds, a heavy pull. It was unlikely that it could have been accidentally discharged.

Churchill had also tested cartridges at various angles and distances. He produced a leather target to show how the spread of pellets was affected by both. The gun had been fired six feet from Williamson. Asked by Dodson if all his experiments were done on leather he replied, 'We do not use human bodies.'

Sir Travers asked, 'Can you understand any way in which a man can hold a gun and the gun be six feet away when it is fired?'

Churchill was sure. 'Three feet would be the limit.'

All of Benton's claims of a scuffle and an accident were negated.

Dodson defended Benton well. He invited the jury to return a verdict of manslaughter, and he might have succeeded had Benton not insisted on going into the witness box to tell and show what happened.

Benton read the oath and the ear tube was produced. Dodson stood in the witness box and shouted questions at him. He asked him if he had occupied his smallholding for twenty-five years.

Benton replied:

*I cannot hear what you are saying. I have never heard one syllable of what any of the gentlemen have said all the time – not one syllable. And I was taken to prison and I have heard nothing at all – nothing at all whatever, and I have done nothing.*

There was laughter at that. Sir Travers reprimanded, 'This is not a laughing matter and if the public cannot constrain themselves from this indecent exhibition I'll have the court cleared. There is nothing funny in a man being tried for his life.'

But privately he was forming his own opinions of Benton, one being that he was 'as dramatic as an actor'.

Benton put the tube in his right ear and said that he could hear better.

Asked if he had felt any ill will towards Williamson for taking his smallholding, he said, 'Not a ha'penny worth. I did not like going out myself, though.'

'Do you remember the occasion of this happening – March 21st?'

'Yes, I know all that happened. It is indelibly printed on my mind, and you can put it in a filbert nutshell if you wrote it on a piece of paper. I saw PC Daw that morning. He knew I was in trouble and had to get out. I was almost out and I had made arrangements with Judd to put two carts in his hovel and me and my wife were going to take the pony to Wisbech market on Saturday and sell it.'

Knowing that Benton's neighbours, and Williamson, were afraid of the way he went about with a cocked gun, Daw had asked him to hand it in. Benton said that he had been on his way to do that when the accident had happened. He had got his gun from Judd's and left it in the middle of a field while he went and had his tea. After tea, he had seen Williamson letting his wife's pony out. They had had words about it, but he had not had his gun. He had gone home and had two cups of tea and then he had decided to take his gun to Daw. He remembered that he had a sheath for it, which he had thrown into a hedge some weeks before, and he went past the stable on his way to get it.

As he passed the stable he saw Williamson with his back to the door, forking straw down under his horse. With his gun under his arm, he had stood in the doorway. When Williamson had turned round and had seen him he had made a grab for the gun.

He had got through that very well and then, at that point, Benton asked for his gun. He would demonstrate what had happened. He would not be prevented. As Sir Travers later wrote, 'Once the prisoner had started no one could stop him. He was oblivious to directions from any quarter and I never felt so completely unable to control a court.'

Benton left the witness box and, as Sir Travers wrote:

*With his gun in his hand and paying no attention to judge or jury he proceeded to demonstrate his story to the only person he could see, who was, in fact, the learned Clerk of Assize. That gentleman was made by*

*Benton to play most unwillingly the part of the victim, the muzzle of the gun being, for most of the time, within a few inches of his head while Benton's finger was playing with the trigger.*

Benton said: 'He got hold of it with his left hand, pulled it up and wriggled it around.' He then repeated the sleeve and bandage reasons for the gun firing. 'He went on his back. And that is all I saw. I bolted from the place, frightened.'

Benton said that he had known Williamson was afraid of the gun, but he denied having said to Haigh that he would shoot anyone who touched his wife.

'He says that you did say it to him.'

'Then he is a fibber and a lord of a fibber. He has got rusty with me. He came down to mine once and asked me to let him have a stone of apples. I put them in a basket and took them up. He turned a bit rusty about it. He thought I was going to give them to him.'

'Do you remember the day on which Williamson was unfortunately shot?'

'Yes, I know nothing else.'

Asked if he had thought that taking his gun past the stable would frighten Williamson, he said: 'I'll tell you. I had an impression in my mind that it would, because it was frightening people.'

'You took it down to frighten him?'

'Yes, nothing else occurred to my mind.'

'When you saw Williamson in the stable door you lifted the muzzle of your gun?'

'I never lifted anything. I stood there about two seconds and was going to fetch this case.'

'How did you get inside the stable?'

'I was not inside. I was just under the eaves. Before you could say knife he was at me.'

Asked again how he thought the gun had gone off, sleeve or bandage, he said it had been a combination of both.

He was then asked, 'Is it right that Mr and Mrs Allen saw you walking up and down with the gun under your arm after they had heard the shot?'

In a statement he had said, 'I was wrong in having the gun after he was shot.'

Now, on trial, he said of Allen's evidence: 'It is the most abominable lie that was ever let out of a man's mouth because he could not see me if he wanted to. I am positive. He owes me £10 now.'

Summing up would not be easy for prosecution, defence or judge. Sir Henry asked the jury for a guilty verdict. Dodson went for an acquittal, stressing that Benton had made no attempt to run but had gone straight to Daw and said that there had been an accident.

'And that is what I ask you to say – that there has been an accident and no crime at all. Feeble and fettered and imperfect as he may be by his physical incapabilities, he has been anxious all along to tell his story of what happened.'

Sir Travers' summing up lasted an hour and then, after a half hour retirement, the jury returned a verdict of guilty, but with a strong recommendation to mercy. He had expected that outcome. 'Almost from the start, we all felt that a conviction for murder would not be followed by an execution. I still thought the jury might wish to reward the old man for his performance by returning a verdict of *non compos mentis*, though no question of insanity had been raised. They no doubt felt that a strong recommendation to mercy would have the same effect.'

Benton believed that he would hang. He said: 'I did not do it, but I shall get to heaven a little bit before my time.'

Sir Travers then passed the death sentence on Benton – twice, because he did not hear what was said the first time and every word had to be repeated.

When he got to the last words the second time, 'May the Lord have mercy on your soul,' Benton said that he was not at all sure of that. 'I don't see why he should.'

*Saturday market place, King's Lynn.* The author

It had been a long day in court. It was a relief to everyone when he was escorted out. Sir Travers no doubt spoke for everyone when he said: 'I was not sorry to see the last of him.'

Benton did not get to heaven a little before his time. He was reprieved almost at once.

Chapter 11

# Battery
# 1930

One afternoon in the late summer of 1914 a Red Cross train of wounded British soldiers who had fought in the great battle at Mons steamed into Cambridge station. In the first carriage, the first man to speak to a reporter from the local Cambridge newspaper was William Hillier, a constable in the Isle of Ely Constabulary who had been called up as a Grenadier Guards reservist.

'Oh I am not hurt much,' was his cheery remark, the reporter quoted. 'I was in the thick of it at Mons and got hurt in the leg.'

Police Sergeant William Hillier was an exemplary officer. He joined the Isle of Ely Constabulary in July 1914 and was transferred to March, in the heart of the Fens, in November 1915 after serving and being wounded in the Great War. He remained there until his transfer back to Ely in May 1923. In February 1926 he was promoted to sergeant and his dedication to his work led everyone to believe that he would be further promoted. In November 1929 that seemed more than likely as it was announced that he was to take charge of the sub-division of Chatteris.

Since his return to Ely, Hillier had made numerous friends, many connected with his off-duty interests. He was fascinated by the area's past and was a member of the Cambridge Antiquarian Society and the Ely Field Club. But his main interest was wireless. He made wireless sets for himself and for others, and he was always glad to repair a set for someone.

One way and another, Hillier was a respected and popular man in the Ely area. It came as an intense shock to everyone, therefore, in January 1930, to hear that he had been dismissed from the force. It was the only topic of conversation and no one could believe it. If such a sober cathedral town could be said to have been rocked by a sensation it was then, and the *Ely Standard* used the word in its headline: ISLE POLICE SENSATION. Ex-police sergeant Hillier had been charged with 'a serious offence'.

# ISLE POLICE SENSATION.

## EX-POLICE SERGEANT HILLIER ADMITS HIS GUILT.

## Crowded Court Listens to Protracted Proceedings.

### PROSECUTING SOLICITOR'S POINTED QUESTIONS.

Within two months of the public announce-ment that he had been promoted to take charge of the sub-division of Chatteris, Police-Sergeant William A. Hillier, who has since been dismissed the Force, appeared at Ely Police Court, yesterday (Thursday), to answer a serious charge.

Hillier, whose name is known throughout the Isle of Ely, had enjoyed a somewhat meteoric rise in the Force, and his constant attention to duty led everyone to believe that he was marked out for still higher pro-motion.

The news of the charge against him created something in the nature of a sensation in Ely, where he has been stationed for the past seven years. In all circles it has been the one topic of discussion, and when first it was made known people, and especially Hillier's more intimate friends, would not attach any credence to it.

*Newspaper headline: Isle Police Sensation.* Cambridgeshire Times

On Thursday 9 January he appeared at Ely Police Court, a court more accustomed to dealing with cases of riding a bike without a light or failure to have a dog licence. The Hillier case was to be heard in the larger of the two courts and it was packed to overflowing as he was seated at his solicitor's table to hear the prosecution allege that he had stolen a wireless battery from Currys Ltd, Ely.

J W A Ollard of Wisbech, prosecuting, began by expressing regret that Hillier had been dismissed from the Constabulary ahead of his trial as it may seem to pre-judge the case. He appreciated the terrible position that Hillier was in, and he had sympathy for him, but the manager of Currys Ltd, Henry John Burton, was also in a terrible position. He would be sacked if his company found him 'short of stock'. He concluded by asking the Bench, who knew Hillier well as a police officer whose word they had often previously accepted in court, to forget all their knowledge of him and to judge the case only on the testimony of witnesses.

The first of those witnesses was Harry Burton. He had managed the Ely shop for two and a half years and, over that time had got to know

*High Street, Ely, today.* The author

Hillier well as a wireless enthusiast and customer. Over the previous year, he told the court, several items had gone missing from the shop and he had told the police. On 21 December, PC Kemp had called in and had marked various wireless articles. Amongst them had been a battery.

On 23 December, Hillier had come into the shop to collect a radiator muff, but he had put it by and had called back for it later. On that second visit Burton had seen him standing near the battery. He had then turned away to serve a customer, Hillier had left, and when he had turned back the marked battery was gone. No one but Hillier could have taken it.

Burton told the police at once and at eleven that night he was asked to go to the police station. Hillier was there, and so was the marked battery. Superintendent Newell asked Burton to identify it as Currys property.

Hillier said: 'I know it came from yours. I took it. Haven't I often taken things from your shop?'

On several occasions Hillier had been allowed to take things and pay for them later, but they were always booked out to him. The battery had not been.

Burton told the court of other items that had gone over the past months – two loudspeakers, and a Lissen Super 60 High Tension Battery valued at fifteen shillings and sixpence. Asked about them Hillier had said:

*I did not take that. I took from the shop the Amphion loudspeaker. It is at my house now. I know where it is. I will fetch it in the morning. I have the Triaton unit at my house I purchased from you six weeks ago for seventeen shillings and sixpence. You see what disgrace I am in and what disgrace it brings on my colleagues!*

PC Kemp then gave evidence that, having heard from Burton, he and Sergeant Baker had searched the Armoury at the police station and had found the marked battery in a deep box. They had watched Hillier go into the Armoury at ten-thirty.

When he left the station he was called back by Baker and asked, 'What have you got under your cape?'

Hillier had replied: 'A battery. I bought it from Currys this evening.'

It had been the marked battery.

Proceedings then took a new course, concentrating on Hillier's health.

K S M Smith, his doctor for four years, told the Bench that he had noticed a change in him over the previous six months. He worried over trivial things.

D F Jackson of King's Lynn, defending Hillier, asked, 'You mean he was abnormal?'

Smith said he believed that he was suffering from nervous exhaustion. Seven and eight months ago he had had two motorcycle

*The present police station. Hillier's station was across the way, adjacent to the Shire Hall.* The author

accidents and had not been himself since. He was 'capable of doing unaccountable things as a result of his nervous state,' but he had examined him the day before yesterday and he had been sane.

Ollard went back to a previous occasion when Smith had seen Hillier, in August, when that might not have been the case. His questioning was unrelenting.

'Was he then sane or mad?'

'He was abnormal.'

'I want to know whether this man was mad or sane.'

'Legally he was sane. Mentally he was abnormal.'

'Could he at that time distinguish right from wrong?'

'I did not ask him. I assume that he did.'

'In August could he distinguish right from wrong?'

'I am only a doctor. I don't go in for psychoanalysis.'

'Did you report any abnormal state of mind to his superintendent?'

'Why should I?'

'Answer the question and don't ask them. Did you report to the superintendent?'

'No, of course I didn't.'

'Was he in August fit to carry out his duties?'

'It is doubtful.'

'Do you think that when Hillier picked the battery up in Currys shop he knew that he was picking it up?'

The laughter in court ended the attack on Smith, who left the witness box, after saying that he believed Hillier had not known what he was doing, stressing that he was not fit to give evidence to the court. It was bad enough that the man was having to sit through the questioning of his sanity.

A second doctor, F H Beckett, followed Smith, to say that from July to November he had treated Hillier for burns he had received in a fire. Other symptoms had led him to believe that if he did not take sick leave he would have a nervous breakdown. His family history, he said, would support that. He had treated his sister for fits for several years and she had recently died in Colney Hatch Asylum. And yes, in response to more of Smith's questioning, 'he could distinguish right from wrong, but at times he should not like to say that he could.'

'Is it your opinion that this man was insane when he took the battery?'

To further laughter, Beckett said, 'I was not present at the time and cannot say what the condition of his brain was.'

Hillier, though plainly ill, had refused to take sick leave, saying that he could not do without work. But work had quickly decided that it could do without him. He had been dismissed. The Bench knew him to be a good man. And, despite Ollard's advice, chose not to overlook that entirely. Superintendent Newell was asked to read a record of Hillier's service in the Grenadier Guards and the Isle of Ely Constabulary, plaudits that were no longer of consequence after all that had been revealed in court.

For the sake of a battery worth fifteen shillings, a man's career and reputation had been hacked to pieces and, in response to the prosecution's pitiless and inept questioning, the state of his mental health had been made public by the town's GPs who, as Smith said, were only doctors and not psychoanalysts. Whatever the outcome, Hillier was a loser.

When the Bench returned with its verdict the Chairman said:

*Sergeant Hillier, we have carefully considered this case and, in our deliberate judgement, we feel that taking into consideration your long service as an officer in the force, that you have been commended from this Bench several times, have served your country well in the war, and then taking into consideration your health and mental condition, we have decided to bind you over for two years. You will pay the court costs, fifteen shillings, and £5 towards the costs of the prosecution – and the battery will be handed over.*

Chapter 12

# Never a Human Being
# 1930

S unday 6 April 1930 was a fine spring day, perfect for a walk beside the river Nene in the fenland town of March. Harry King, a railway platelayer who lived in the town's Nene Parade, thought so. He had strolled along the north bank to just beyond the Nene junction railway bridge, the Iron Bridge, when he saw a box in the water. It was floating end up and it was near to the bank. He could reach it. He pulled it out and cut the string that was around it. There was a brown paper wrapping and he used a stick to move that aside and partly lift the lid. The box contained a towel, with something wrapped in it. What he saw when he moved the towel was a baby's hand.

*Narrow boat about to pass under March town bridge to reach the part of the River Nene by Nene Parade.* The author

*Nene Parade, March.* The author

Immediately, he left the box where it was and went for the police. He found PC Williams in Broad Street and told him of his find. Perhaps strangely, he was taken to March police station to make a statement to Superintendent Norman. Only when that had been done did he and the constable go back to the river and the box.

*Broad Street, March.* The author

Williams opened the box and moved the towel and yes, it was there all right. He saw its hand, and its head. He replaced the towel, put the box in a sack he had brought for the purpose, and took it to the police station.

Once there, in the presence of King and Williams, it was Sergeant Connor's turn to open the box. He took the little body out. There were no external marks of violence, and no identification marks on either the baby or its container. All that was discovered was that the baby had been a girl.

Within an hour, Dr Patrick Joseph Smith of Gordon Avenue in March arrived and he too examined the body. He saw no marks, but a post-mortem would have to be carried out to determine the cause of death.

On Tuesday 8 April, two days after that gruesome discovery in the Nene, an inquest took place at March police station. The coroner was F W Dawbarn of Wisbech. Also attending was A E Crowson, the Registrar of Births and Deaths for the March district.

King and Williams gave evidence, and then it was the turn of Dr Smith.

The coroner asked him, 'Had the child ever an independent existence from its mother?'

'No, sir.'

'Then it was stillborn?'

'Yes, sir.'

'In that case then it is useless to ask you whether the post-mortem showed whether the death was due to drowning or not?'

'That is so. There was no water in the lungs which showed that it had not a separate existence.'

'Was it a full time child?'

'Yes, sir. But it is evident that it did not receive qualified medical attention at birth.'

'What you have told us, of course, does away with any question of murder, for I had feared myself that that might be the case. Now nothing further concerns us.'

The coroner, obviously relieved, told the jury that their labours had been lightened in a very pleasant manner. He had been very much afraid, before the inquest opened, that it might prove to be a case of murder by some person or persons unknown. But Dr Smith had made it clear that the child never lived apart from its mother, it had been stillborn, and therefore was never a human being. The only offence committed appeared to be concealment of birth, and that was a police matter.

It would be up to the police to discover the identity of the child and the mother, which would lead to the identity of the person who had put the box in the Nene. In his opinion, it would not be an easy task in 'these days of motor cars'. The person may not be from March. It might have been someone who had thought March was as good or perhaps better than the one where the birth took place in which to dispose of it.

Finding the baby's mother, however, proved to be an easier task than expected. Too many people were aware that she had given birth, and had no baby, for her to remain unnamed.

Madeleine Francessa Ballantyne, a twenty-five-year-old cook at the *George Hotel* in Chatteris, was committed from March Petty Sessions on 26 April, charged that by secretly disposing of the dead body of a female child, which she had given birth to on 28 February, she had endeavoured to conceal its birth.

Charged with her was a twenty-three-year-old law student, Harold Howard, of Creek Road, March. It was said that he had unlawfully carried out the secret disposal of the dead body of the female child which had been delivered to Ballantyne by placing it in the Nene at March.

Ballantyne and Howard came before Mr Justice Macnaghton when the Cambridgeshire Assizes opened at the Shire Hall, Cambridge, at the end of May. They both pleaded guilty.

The story of the young couple was outlined for the Grand Jury by prosecutor Linton Thorp.

They had met in London in June 1929. Howard had been there to take his intermediate law examination. When he went back to March, to his then home in Nene Parade, she went with him. Unable to afford her keep, he had found her a job as a cook in the vicarage at Yaxley, near Peterborough. It had been there that she had given birth to their baby.

Howard was with a Wisbech firm of solicitors, Ollard and Ollard. Ballantyne sent him a telegram there to tell him that the birth had taken place, and it seemed obvious from its cryptic wording that it had been pre-arranged. It read: SPECIAL ARRIVED. COLLECT TONIGHT. MADELEINE.

Howard went from Wisbech to Yaxley to collect the body of his child, already wrapped in its cardboard box, paper and string. He then took it to March and threw it in the Nene.

Linton Thorp stayed with the telegram. The couple, before the event he thought, had seemed to be prepared for it to be dead. The telegram was very suggestive and needed some explanation.

The judge did not agree. He felt that the fact that the child had been stillborn 'negated any suspicion'.

But Linton Thorp was not convinced. 'It would appear to do so. It was clear, however, that the prisoners were anticipating the birth and that they anticipated disposing of whatever was born in whatever state it was born.'

He was overruled and the case moved on. Two character witnesses appeared for Ballantyne. Reverend Ernest O'Connor, the vicar of Yaxley, said that she had been in his service from July 1929 to 3 March 1930 and had been honest, kind, obliging and a good worker. She had left the vicarage after the birth, but she had soon found other employment, at the *George Hotel*, Chatteris. Its owner, William Coleman, was as pleased with Ballantyne as O'Connor. She was a quiet, honest, capable and willing girl. She was very satisfactory in all her duties and if she was acquitted he would continue to employ her.

But what of Harold Howard?

J W A Ollard, an ex-mayor of Wisbech, was called to give evidence that Howard had been articled to his brother, K deH Ollard. He was illegitimate, and the matter of his birth had been a consideration when he entered the legal profession. But he had done well, passing the intermediate examination he had taken at the time he had met Ballantyne. His final would have been taken in June 1931.

Those weighted words – would have been – told what Howard's future was to be. And he had tried so hard to make something of himself, to overcome his poor circumstances and to 'raise himself up into a different sphere of life to what his environment was'.

And what an environment. His home life had been unhappy and he had not had much affection. Until the age of nine, when he had gone to live with grandparents, 'he had not the refining influence of a home or of a mother'. At thirteen, he and his mother had gone to live in March and his ambition had become to 'advance himself out of his position into one of respect and esteem.' He had managed to be taken on by Ollard and had done splendidly, but at times seemed depressed and unhappy. He had had infantile paralysis as a child and had been left with a limp, making him unable to enjoy sports with his friends and perhaps earn their regard. But he had been brave.

Howard's past was one of gritty determination to make something of himself against the odds. His future was now doubtful. His articles with Ollard and Ollard had been cancelled and it had become a question of whether the Law Society would allow him to continue in the profession. If not convicted, he may manage to transfer his articles, or he might get a job as a clerk – but in another part of the country.

All concerned agreed that the case was an unusual one, full of foolishness. Howard had stood by the girl and had shown manly spirit, getting himself into the fix he was in even though he had known that it would affect his future. He might one day have been sitting in that very court, instructing counsel, but now his entire career was at an end.

Ballantyne's actions had been in ignorance of their seriousness, and to hide her shame. There had been no attempt to hide her pregnancy. She had told the district nurse, and Mrs O'Connor. It had been hoped that she could go into the Ely Diocesan Maternity Home in Cambridge for the birth, but there had not been a vacancy. And then, at the vicarage, she had had a bad fall downstairs.

Because of that Ballantyne had been certain that the baby would be stillborn and she had got it into her head that it would be an offence to try to get a stillborn child buried in consecrated ground. O'Connor might have reassured her on that, but he was not consulted. She had thought that it was up to herself to dispose of the body as best she could and, believing that, she had sent the telegram to Howard.

J P Gorman defended Ballantyne well. It seemed to him that, considering her state of mind and her dreadful predicament, justice could be served just as well by not imprisoning her but by letting her go back to her job at the *George Hotel*.

Justice Macnaghton said that both prisoners had pleaded guilty to the concealment of a birth, an offence which deserved severe punishment, and had been found guilty, but the circumstances were such that he could take a merciful view. Both prisoners had suffered very much and he had come to the conclusion that justice would be met if they were both bound over in their own recognisance of £10 each to be of good behaviour in the future.

Ballantyne went back to her job at the *George*.

## Chapter 13

# No Mercy for Mrs Major
# 1934

## *Warning: It is recommended that you do not read this while eating corned beef.*

Ethel Lillie Major was the daughter of a Lincolnshire game-keeper who, at the age of twenty-four, had given birth to an illegitimate daughter. Ethel's parents raised Auriol as their own and everyone was to believe that the girls were sisters.

Ethel's husband did. In 1918, when Auriol was three, Ethel married Arthur Major, a lorry driver, and they shared her parents' home near Horncastle. As far as Arthur knew, Auriol was Ethel's little sister, and it was only in 1929, when they moved to a home of their own in the nearby hamlet of Kirkby-on-Bain, that the local gossips enlightened him.

Ethel was a bad-tempered woman, arrogant and boastful, who was not popular. The information harmed the marriage, but it was already failing. The couple argued, and went on arguing, going on to threats and violence. They reached a stage where they hated each other, but they stayed together, miserably, into the mid-May of 1934, when Ethel was forty-two and Arthur forty-eight. She announced then that she had found two anonymous love letters to her husband.

She said that they had been written by a neighbour, Rose Kettleborough, and she told everyone so. Even the chief constable of Lincolnshire. Even Rose's husband. To him she said: 'Have you any idea that your wife is writing letters to my husband and hiding them in hedges?' He did not believe her and accused her of always 'watching and prying about,' another side to her unattractive personality.

She went on to tell her doctor, and showed him the letters, saying, 'A man like him is not fit to live. I will do him in,' and, on 19 May, she told a local police officer. To him she added that her husband had given her a cup of tea one morning and had put something in it to get rid of her.

Ethel, by then, had left home and had gone to stay with her father a few miles away, taking her fifteen-year-old son, Lawrence, with her.

She had been extravagant in her marriage, spending too much on herself, especially on clothes, and not paying day-to-day bills. Arthur had had enough of it. He went to the *Horncastle News* and arranged for a notice to be printed in the 26 May edition stating that he would not be responsible for her debts.

Not a wise action when Ethel's thoughts were on 'doing him in'.

During the evening of 22 May, Arthur ate a meal of corned beef. He did not enjoy it. It tasted off. There was no way he could eat it all so he took his plate outside and gave the leavings to Mr Maltby's wire-haired terrier next door.

Within hours, Arthur became extremely ill. Ethel stayed with him, but she did not call a doctor. It was her father, Tom Brown, calling by later, who sent Lawrence for the doctor.

The doctor who came had never attended the family before, so it was up to Ethel to put him in the picture. Arthur often had fits, she told him. He had suffered from epilepsy for years. Had the doctor known that Arthur was a lorry driver he may have questioned that,

*Lincolnshire Police headquarters, Lincoln.* The author

but he believed Ethel. He found Arthur foaming at the mouth and unable to communicate. Sweat was running from him and his skin had a blue tinge. He was having fits.

The doctor's treatment eased his agony, and he was a little better the next day, but in the evening he had a relapse, suffering agonising muscular contractions and convulsion after convulsion. At about seven, with his father-in-law, son and wife at his bedside, Arthur managed to say that he was thirsty. Ethel fetched a glass of water, raising him in her arms. Tom Brown supported him while he drank. Three hours later he was writhing in agony, but was able to murmur, 'I'm going to die.' One more hour and then, at ten-forty, after forty-eight hours of suffering, Arthur was dead.

His widow had no time for grief. She began rather feverish activity. She asked the doctor for a death certificate. He made one out for status epilepticus. She visited the undertaker and demanded burial as quickly as possible, within three days. He was taken aback, but the funeral was arranged for 27 May.

And that would have been that, Arthur despatched at express speed, but for a letter received by Inspector Dodson of the Lincolnshire Constabulary, Horncastle:

*Sir, Have you ever heard of a wife poisoning her husband? Look further into the death of Mr Major of Kirkby-on-Bain. Why did he complain of his food tasting nasty and throw it to a neighbour's dog, which has since died? Ask the undertaker if he looked natural after death. Why did he stiffen so quickly? Why was he so jerky when dying? I myself have heard her threaten to poison him years ago. In the name of the law, I beg you to analyse the contents of his stomach.*

It was signed 'Fairplay'.

But for Fairplay, who was never traced, foul play would not have been suspected. Dodson checked it out. He went to see Arthur's doctor and heard enough of his sudden illness to call on the coroner in Spilsby. An order was issued to stop the funeral. The grave was dug, mourners had gathered in the Majors' home, Arthur was there in his coffin, and then, suddenly, he was gone, whisked away for a post-mortem. With him went the terrier from next door, unearthed at twilight from Mr Maltby's garden.

Organs from the bodies of man and dog were sent to Home Office pathologist, Roche Lynch, at St Mary's, Paddington. Perhaps for the first time in his distinguished career he was to examine the remains of a terrier.

His investigations established beyond doubt that both had been poisoned with strychnine. Lynch believed that Arthur had been given two doses, the second shortly before his death, probably in a liquid. Strychnine, the cruellest poison of all, was excessively bitter and, in his opinion, 'no suicide would choose it, and certainly not for a second time, because no one except a madman would take a second dose after suffering all the agony of a first administration.'

Knowing that he had a murder on his hands Dodson called in Scotland Yard, and Chief Inspector Hugh Young, later CID Commander at the Yard, arrived in Horncastle on 2 July. Young was to remember it as a sunny summer day.

He began by finding out all that he could about the Majors and their life together. Important to him were an apparent penchant of Ethel's for sending and receiving anonymous letters and the fact that the notice which was to have appeared in the Horncastle paper on the 26th was cancelled by Ethel on the 25th, the day after Arthur's death. Could Ethel's knowledge of that public notice have decided Arthur's fate?

As investigations continued, several seemingly unconnected small details began to weave themselves into a mesh of suspicion of Ethel Major, whose signed statements varied. On 3 July Young called on Lawrence Major in Horncastle and then he went to meet Ethel.

He was already suspicious enough of her to give her a formal caution before the interview began. He found her to be cool and not suffering sorrow at the loss of her husband. She seemed quite callous as she told him that she 'felt much better in health since he was gone'.

And then she said that the corned beef Arthur had eaten had caused his death. She was to become obsessed with corned beef. She stressed that she had nothing to do with providing Arthur's meals, she and her son had gone to her father's two weeks before his death. And then it was the corned beef again. 'My husband bought his tinned beef himself,' she insisted. 'I know that I never bought any. I hate corned beef and I think it is a waste of money to buy such rubbish.'

Ethel's father, who had retired from gamekeeping, had used poisons on vermin, and still had them. Young moved on to that. Did she know that he had poisons? A leading question as she had been living in his house at the time of Arthur's death.

'I did not know where he kept the poison,' she said, and then came a mistake. 'I never at any time had poison in the house, and I did not know that my husband died of strychnine poisoning.'

Only Roche Lynch, Hugh Young and a few high-ranking police officers knew what had killed Arthur. And yet Mrs Major knew.

'I never mentioned strychnine,' Young challenged. 'How did you know that your husband died of poisoning by strychnine?'

'Oh – I'm sorry,' she said, calmly. 'I must have made a mistake. I am still of the opinion that he died from poison from the corned beef.'

Back to the corned beef. Although, of course, she had nothing to do with her husband's meals.

'I have never bought corned beef, nor has my son.' But she had seen some on the pantry shelf, ready for that last fateful meal. She said that it had been black, quite bad, but she had not told Arthur.

To Young, her unconcern for his well-being seemed not far from a state of mind that could contemplate poison.

At that point Ethel had got up and said to Young, 'You look tired. Let me make you a cup of tea.'

The idea, strangely, had no appeal. 'No, thank you.'

She had smiled, unembarrassed. 'You needn't be afraid of me. I wont put anything in it.'

Although he regretted it, Lawrence had not had a happy life with his warring parents, Young knew that he had to interview the boy for a second time, in his mother's presence. Twenty years later, he wrote in his memoirs:

*I can recall even now her agitation and anger when the lad related how, a day or two before his father was taken ill, his mother had sent him out to buy a tin of corned beef for his father's meal.*

She had denied it, heatedly. But Lawrence persisted. 'Don't you remember giving me the money to go and get it?'

'No, I didn't. Your father sent you.' Lawrence stuck to it. His father had been out and, anyway, the woman in the shop remembered it clearly.

Ethel had then erupted into a violent rage and shouted, 'Every woman in this village is a liar.'

She knew the significance of what Lawrence had said. To everyone she had sworn that she had no connection with Arthur's meals – and her son had said that she had. Young wrote: 'It was one of those slips which so often prove the downfall of the most cunning criminal.'

The only thing left to prove to give Young a case against Ethel Major was access to strychnine. Her father kept a locked trunk in his bedroom. In it was an hexagonal green bottle of strychnine crystals. Young had every sympathy for the old man, patently honest, as he asked, 'Did your daughter know the whereabouts of the box?'

'Yes, mister.'

'Would your daughter be able to open this box?'

'No, mister.' Brown showed Young the cloth belt that he always wore with the key to the box in a buttoned pocket. 'I always carry the key of that box about with me in this pocket. It has never left me, day or night.'

But Young felt that, somehow, Ethel must have opened that box. While he puzzled that out, he went on to the love letters, which he believed had been written by Ethel. The writing was disguised, but there were similarities to an anonymous letter received by the Lincolnshire force's chief constable on 12 May saying that Arthur Major was a drink driver who should be taken off the road 'for the safety of the people in the village'. And in one of the love letters was the wording, 'Letters are nice dear but some day I shall be able to have your arms around me for always.'

Young called again on an Ethel still keen to blame Rose Kettleborough. Rose, she said, had had access to her husband, her pantry and the corned beef. Young let her have her say, and then he had his 'Columbo' moment. He was leaving, but just a moment. One more thing. Would she mind writing down a few words for him? How about always? And people?

There was a beautiful pink and gold sunset when Young knocked on the Majors' cottage door on 9 July. After a week, he was ready. He followed Ethel into the small front room where he cautioned her and said that he had come to detain her for the murder of her husband.

She was amazed. 'I loved my husband and I am his lawful wedded wife.'

She had detested him, showed only malice towards him, had been unconcerned at his death, and yet – she had loved him. Young took her to Horncastle where she was formally charged and remanded.

For Young, there was one loose end to tie up before he could be on his way back to Scotland Yard. He made a thorough search of Ethel's home. It took a long time, but he knew what he was looking for, the only thing needed to convict Ethel Major of murder.

In her bedroom, in a wardrobe crammed with new dresses and twenty new pairs of expensive shoes, he found a brown suitcase. In it was a white sheet, some clothing – and a purse. In the purse were some documents proving that the purse had been used recently, a penny wrapped in paper with the words Mother's Penny on it – and a key.

Young put the key onto a large bunch and went to see Tom Brown. 'Did you ever have another key for the trunk?'

'What have you found now?' He looked sad and apprehensive. 'I am an old man, mister. I will tell you nothing but the truth. I did have another key, but I lost it years ago. I never knew the going of it.'

*Lincoln Castle, close to the Cathedral.* The author

Young passed the bunch of keys to Brown. Reluctantly, he picked one out. 'That's her, mister.'

And that was it. The final link in the chain of evidence that was to prove the guilt of Ethel Major.

*The Crown Court in the grounds of Lincoln Castle, surrounded by the city's Christmas Market.* The author

When she came up for trial at Lincoln Assizes on 29 October 1934 her neighbours in Horncastle and Kirkby-on-Bain organised a day trip. A coachload of them turned up at the court but, perhaps because of their picnic air, they were refused admission.

Without their support, but defended by leading attorney Norman Birkett KC, she appeared before Mr Justice Charles, looking frail, her brown dress doing nothing to enliven her sallow complexion. In a low, firm voice she pleaded not guilty.

The prosecution detailed the case against Ethel. The blameless Rose Kettleborough gave evidence, as did Auriol, Tom Brown and Roche Lynch. Although he must have known from the start that he had no case for the defence, Birkett tried, but the evidence against Ethel was overwhelming. As prosecutor Richard O'Sullivan KC said: 'The case is really, on the evidence, unanswerable.'

Ethel Major sensed the approach of the inevitable. She sobbed and hid her face against a woman prison officer. As Judge Charles summed up she seemed on the verge of collapse. Her head went down and she slumped forwards and had to be prevented from falling on the floor. A doctor was brought while the judge just carried on regardless.

When the jury of nine men and three women returned with their verdict in little over an hour, Norman Birkett, who the following year was to defend double murderer Dr Buck Ruxton with as little hope of success, knew that he had lost.

As she was sentenced to death, Ethel broke down completely and had to be carried from the dock, her wails echoing through the silent court and down the corridors beyond, growing fainter and fainter as she was taken away, until no sound could be heard.

She spent the time awaiting her execution in prison in Hull, where she was to be hanged on 19 December. The jury had made a strong recommendation to mercy and expectation was high that she would not die, but the days passed without that expectation being fulfilled. The recommendation had been passed on to the appropriate quarter, but poisoners who had shown no mercy to their victims, who had heartlessly watched them suffer and die, were not often allowed to avoid their day of reckoning.

Many people in Hull, women especially, found her imprisonment in the city upsetting and hoped for a reprieve. Such was the concern, that the city's Lord Mayor, Alderman S Stark, felt compelled to make an eleventh hour appeal for mercy the day before she was due to keep her appointment with Tom Pierrepoint, the executioner. He had left it so late because he had been sure the jury's appeal would be acted upon. It had not been and, on 18 December, he sent a telegram to the Home Secretary, John Gilmour. It read that it was distressing the great city's 300,000 inhabitants, it was near Christmas, it was for humanity.

Copies were sent to the prime minister, to the MPs for Hull, and to George Lansbury, the labour MP and social reformer, founder of the *Daily Herald* – although today his granddaughter, the actress Angela Lansbury, is better known.

It was most usual for a prisoner to be reprieved under the Royal Prerogative of Mercy, exercised by the Home Secretary on behalf of the monarch, so Stark sent another telegram, to the King and Queen. As the minutes ticked away to nine o'clock, the time of the execution, Stark still hoped to receive word of a reprieve. When he spoke to a reporter at his home at eight-fifteen, he said: 'I have not yet entirely given up hope, although there does not seem much possibility of a favourable reply at this late hour.'

There was none. At eight-thirty, Ethel was with a prison chaplain. She did not break down as she had on hearing her death sentence. At nine, she went bravely to the drop, a perfection of the effective long drop introduced by Calcraft's successor, William Marwood, a Horncastle man.

Uncle and nephew, Tom and Albert Pierrepoint, known around prisons as 'Uncle Tom and Our Albert,' had seen Ethel the day before and had worked out that she needed a drop of eight feet six inches. It was a fine art, snapping the spinal column, and Tom was master of it, taking only twelve seconds to prepare the prisoner and pull the lever. Apprentice Albert had never executed a woman but he was reassured by Tom. 'I shall be very surprised if Mrs Major isn't calmer than any man you've seen so far.' And he was right. She had not been calm in court at Lincoln, but she would be on the scaffold at Hull.

*Headline: Mrs Major Pays Penalty.* Cambridge Daily News

---

# MRS. MAJOR PAYS PENALTY

## Last Half Hour Spent With Chaplain

M RS. ETHEL LILLIE MAJOR (42), who was sentenced to death for poisoning her husband, a lorry driver, with strychnine, was hanged at Hull Prison to-day. She was the first woman to be executed in this country for eight years.

Mrs. Major spent the last half hour of her life with the prison Chaplain, and bore up bravely when she was conducted to the scaffold.

### HOPE UNTIL THE LAST.

Until a few minutes before the time fixed for the execution (9 a.m.), the Lord Mayor of Hull (Alderman A. Stark) was waiting and hoping for some communication from the Home Secretary which would say that Mrs. Major should not hang.

When a reporter spoke to him at his home at 8.15 a.m. he said: "I have not yet entirely given up hope, although there does not seem much possibility of a favourable reply at this late hour.

"Late last night I received a message from Buckingham Palace that my telegram to the King and Queen had been forwarded to the Home Secretary, but I have received no intimation from Sir John Gilmour."

In his telegram to the King and Queen, Alderman Stark said "The impending execution is giving great distress to thousands of our women, and it is earnestly pleaded that Her Majesty may use her influence in mercy being shown at this eleventh hour to a woman and a mother."

### NO INCIDENTS.

There was a crowd of 300 people outside the prison, but there was no incidents. Women were fewer in number than men among the crowd. Many of the men were dock labourers.

The execution was attended by the Under-Sheriff of Lincolnshire (Mr. Reginald Scorrer), and the executioner was Pierrepoint.

The customary notice announcing that judgment of death had been carried out and also the certificate of the prison surgeon were posted on the prison wall at the entrance gates shortly after nine.

Soon afterwards, the Under-Sheriff, the Governor (Capt. E. D. Roberts), the Rev. W. N. Fraser, assistant chaplain, and Dr. R. J. Barlee, prison medical officer, passed through the wicket gate to the Governor's house. There was a rush by the crowd to read the official notices. People afterwards quickly dispersed.

### INQUEST.

At the inquest a verdict of "death by judicial hanging" was returned.

Capt. Roberts, the Governor, stated that the execution was carried out in a humane and expeditious manner. There was no hitch.

Dr. Barlee stated that death was instantaneous.

The last woman to be hanged in Britain was Mrs. Louie Calvert, who was executed at Strangeways Prison, Manchester, on June 24th, 1926, for the murder of her landlady.

Other women who have been executed include Mrs. Thomson, of Ilford (convicted with Bywaters for the murder of her husband). She was hanged in 1923.

And so Ethel Lillie Major, the last person to be hung at Hull, joined the select coterie of women to be executed in England and Wales in the twentieth century. There was no mercy for the gamekeeper's daughter from Lincolnshire but, as protest gathered pace, there would one day be mercy for all.

She is said to haunt her burial place, Hull prison.

## Chapter 14

# Down to Earth
# 1940–1941

Through World War Two, the people of the Fens fought their own war, that of raising agricultural production time and again to overcome the food shortages caused by U-boat action against incoming supply ships.

It became vital that all land must be farmed and, in 1940, farmers were told that every scrap of land was to be put to the plough. The farmers of the Fens responded, and would go on doing so to the end of the war. In 1940, 112,000 extra acres went into cultivation and, in 1941, Norfolk exceeded its quota of 20,000 extra acres.

That intense activity meant hard work for an army of farm labourers, helped by Land Army girls. Many of the men had served in World War One and were too old for enlistment, or were exempt for a variety of other reasons.

Vital as their work was to the survival of Britain, many of those men felt that they were not playing their part in the defence of their country. They wanted to be nearer to the sharp end of hostilities. Their chance to really be involved came with the formation of the Home Guard in May 1940, just before a wide area of Cambridgeshire suffered its first Luftwaffe bombing raid, with nine people killed in Cambridge and one in Ely.

With the shock of that sweeping through the Fens, men between the ages of seventeen and sixty-five volunteered for the new Home Guard in droves. Ten times the expected number signed up to march about their fields and villages, their enthusiasm making up for their lack of uniforms and arms.

And they were given an important role. The flat, open fenlands, surrounded by RAF airfields, might have been made for the silent drop of parachutes bringing in enemy agents. They were to be on the lookout for German spies.

Tom Cousins was a forty-six-year-old ploughman who had fought for his country in the Great War and joined the Home Guard in

*Church Street, Willingham, at the start of World War Two.* Cambridgeshire Collection

Willingham, a village towards the edge of the Cambridgeshire fens. On the morning of 21 September 1940, he was cycling to work at Glebe Farm. It was early, about seven, so he was surprised to see two men in uniform walking towards him. Strangers on a fen road at that hour were unusual – as were their uniforms. He got off his bike and decided he would have a little chat.

The men looked tired, as if they had not had a good night's sleep. They might have looked better if they had had a shave. One of them, the one with glasses, was limping.

He answered his 'Good morning.' The other man stayed silent. He said that he had hurt his ankle falling into a ditch. They were Danish, in the Danish Army – see, they wore Danish uniforms – and they were based in Cambridge. They were making their way back there, but they were hungry. Was there a shop in Willingham where they could buy food?

Cousins directed them and then he cycled on, uneasily. With the fall of France in June, the fear of invasion had been heightened and those men could be anybody from anywhere, no matter what they said. By the time he got to Glebe Farm he was certain that more than their uniforms had been strange about them.

His Home Guard major was Jack Langton, landlord of the *Three Tuns* in Willingham. He was on his way as soon as he got Cousins' phone call. Together they drove into the village and there, in front of May's Stores, were the two men.

Time for Private Tom Cousins of the Home Guard to have another little chat with them – or with the one who talked – while Langton phoned RAF Oakington. They were still chatting about this and that when a jeep pulled up and guards invited the two to take a ride. They did look tired, after all.

And they *were* German spies. That was soon established. During the previous night they had parachuted into Fen Field, near Glebe Farm, from a circling Heinkel III. They had buried their parachutes and radios, had made a late night call at a mobile home, where they had got directions to Willingham and a cup of tea, and had then spent the dark hours in a field, trying to sleep.

Nothing was ever revealed about the silent spy, but the word was that, within a few days, he had hung himself at Oakington. The other man was Wulf Schmidt, a Dane who had accidentally got involved in spying for the Nazis when he had applied for a job as a linguist. Once in, it had become impossible to get out, but he was a reluctant spy and no Nazi. Within weeks, he had found himself in a Heinkel in a Danish uniform and carrying Danish papers – plus British ones in the name of Harold Williamson.

Schmidt's reluctance to serve Hitler's cause came through in interrogation at Oakington. So much so that he was given a choice – be hung as a spy or become a double agent.

*RAF Oakington.* Cambridgeshire Collection

He made his choice. His radio was unearthed from the fen and, three weeks later, he made his first transmission to Germany. He was to send over one thousand bogus messages, feeding the enemy false information through to the end of the war. He was considered such a super spy that Hitler, via his radio, decorated him with the Iron Cross.

In February 1941, as Schmidt's fiction was making its way from fen to führer, two farm workers were crossing a field at Dovehouse Farm, Ramsey Hollow. It was just after eight o'clock on a cold, frosty morning. Suddenly, they heard three shots, coming from a clump of trees.

Like the fen tigers they were, they went straight in, and there was a parachute and, under it, a man holding a Luger automatic. He could have shot them, but he needed them. His leg had been broken as he landed and he was in agony. He threw his gun aside and, in halting English, told them that he had nothing at all to do with the war – although he did happen to be a German, from Hamburg. The matter was decided when he was found to have with him a powerful wireless transmitter, a torch which could send flashing signals, and a map of nearby RAF Upwood, home to two Blenheim bomber training squadrons.

Unlike Wulf Schmidt, Josef Jakobs was a wholehearted Nazi prepared to live or die for the cause and, over his months in captivity, he never considered a plea for mercy. His court martial at the Duke of York barracks in Chelsea was short and sharp. He was found guilty of espionage and was taken to the Tower of London to await execution.

On the morning of 15 August 1941, Jakobs faced a firing squad of Scots Guardsmen aiming at a piece of white linen pinned to his shirt and, at twelve minutes past seven, he lay dead, the only man to be shot at the Tower in World War Two.

Two Nazi spies had been found in the Fens, but they and their futures could hardly have been more different. Jakobs gave his life for the Third Reich. Schmidt, the famous double agent, or plain Harold Williamson as he became, made England his home. He died in a London hospital in 1992, aged eighty-one.

At the most dangerous time Britain had ever endured the farm labourers of the Fens worked for the war effort in more ways than one. They put millions more acres into cultivation to feed the nation, and they defended their own against all comers. Perhaps it is only fitting that the BBC comedy series *Dad's Army*, featuring a fictional Home Guard unit, should be filmed in Norfolk, but the reality was more tragedy than comedy.

## Chapter 15

# For Love or Money
# 1956

Arthur John Johnson, a single man in his fifties, farmed at Farcet Fen, in the fenland between Yaxley and Whittlesey, an area of dark fields divided by ditches and dykes and crossed by rough tracks and droves. For all its openness, it was not an easy place to get about, especially at night. Unless you knew the place, of course.

Johnson was awkward around women. He had lived with his mother until her death in 1944, and had then had two housekeepers. He was a kind, jolly, contented man. Crowtree Farm, for all its isolation, suited him, and he was a good farmer. Though more at ease with men, he got on well with his second housekeeper, Eileen May Clarke.

Bessie, as she was usually called, was young and pretty. She was married to Morris Arthur Clarke, a fen boy in his twenties, born at Thorney, but he was doing his National Service in the Royal Artillery in the early 1950s and the job at Crowtree brought in a bit of money while she cared for their small daughter.

They got on so well that when Morris Clarke finished his National Service in 1952 the young family moved into Crowtree Farm with Johnson. Clarke, inevitably known as Nobby, was given work on the farm. It was a nice little set up, though the farmhouse could have been more homely. It was damp and smelled musty, and dry rot had taken hold.

Clarke had not been at the farm long when the rumours began. Even miles from anywhere, in the heart of fenland, there were still rumours. He was told that Johnson and Bessie were having an affair which had started while he had been away in the army. He needed little convincing. He thought himself that they were too close.

Bessie denied that anything was going on, but Clarke refused to stay on at Crowtree. He took out a £1,750 mortgage and moved his family the few miles into Peterborough, to a house in Fulbridge Road. He bought a lorry and began his own haulage business.

*Fulbridge Road, Peterborough, now crossed by the Soke Parkway.* The author

It seemed a good move, into a lively town a world away from the bleak fen, and Clarke had the chance to work for his own future. But Bessie really did like Johnson and missed his company. He was living alone and she and her sister used to go to the farm to spend evenings with him when Clarke was working. Johnson often went out, getting into his old grey Morris van to drive to the *Greyhound* in Peterborough for a smoke and a drink or two, but he was as content staying home when his visitors came. They played dominoes.

Johnson liked the Clarkes' little daughter. He was a generous man – he never talked business but he was thought to be well-off – and he liked to treat her. And, despite a smouldering resentment at that supposed relationship, Clarke was prepared to share that generosity.

After two years, his haulage business was not going well and, in October 1956, his debts were mounting. When he asked Johnson to loan him £100 it was given at once, willingly.

But he needed more than £100. His lorry needed repairs costing £600, and other debts amounted to as much again. There was no way that he could find the money and he was forced, at last, to sell his lorry. Peterborough was a railway centre. He got a job as a shunter driver, working mostly at night, but he still liked to hang out with his lorry driver mates.

He spent the evening of 15 October with some of them at the Bishops Road car park. He and Bessie had argued and he had gone off in a mood. His debts, his need for money, worried him constantly. Earlier that day he had been told by his bank that a cheque of his, for £200, had bounced. And there was Johnson. Whatever was going on between Johnson and Bessie was breaking up his marriage, deny it as she might. The two things, love and money, were making him agitated and very angry.

That night, fired by his suspicions and his debts, he decided that it was time to get one thing, at least, sorted out. He would tackle Johnson about Bessie. About ten o'clock, after telling his mates that he was going to see Arthur Johnson at Crowtree Farm, he pedalled off on Bessie's bike.

In the light from the farmhouse, Johnson saw Clarke arrive. He was pleased but surprised as he went out to meet him, saying, 'Hello Nobby, what are you doing here?'

The reply that he got was not one that he could have had any reason to expect.

Just before six o'clock the next morning Ian Macdonald Gordon, who lived at the Barracks in Farcet Fen, was on his way to work when he noticed a small grey Morris van, registration OEW 241, in Two Pope Drove. It was an out-of-the-way spot, two and a half miles from Crowtree, no more than a track to nowhere. It was not the sort of place where anyone would park a vehicle. It struck him as so unusual that he called the police.

Inspector Curtis, based at Stanground, was soon there. In the back of the van he found a large amount of blood and ordered a check on the van's registration. Later that morning the police at Stanground received another phone call. It was from Colin Arthur Muncaster, a forty-one-year-old company director of Woodhall Spa, close to Ethel Major's Kirkby-on-Bain. He was Johnson's cousin and the two men saw each other regularly, often enough for someone at the farm to phone him to say that Johnson was not about. He had gone to the farm at once and what he had seen there, in the yard and in the farmhouse, had made him make the call.

There was blood in the yard, and a trail of blood to the empty outbuilding where the van was kept. From the quantity of blood there, and in the van, the police had great doubts that Johnson was still alive.

The farmhouse had been found unlocked with the door open and the lights on. There was a bit of the *Marie Celeste* about it, as if Johnson had suddenly, for some unknown reason, gone out into the yard. His jacket was there, and his spectacles. And there were three wrappers, such as banks put around wads of notes. They found his wallet. In it was the name Bessie Clarke, and an address in Peterborough. They wondered if she might be a girlfriend. She was checked, but turned out to be his ex-housekeeper.

On 18 October New Scotland Yard was called in and Detective Superintendent Edmund Wilfrid Daws took over what was being treated as a murder enquiry and the search was on for Johnson's body and for his killer.

On 25 October, ten days after Johnson's disappearance, a Peterborough schoolteacher, Malin McCarthy, was fishing at Glassmoor Bank in the heart of fenland, near Whittlesey. He was not having much luck and he decided to go further along, into Bevill's Leam.

What he found there he told at the inquest into Johnson's death at Whittlesey Town Hall on Tuesday 30 October:

> *After going along about fifty yards, I noticed something in the water. This was at about five minutes to one. I saw it was a body of a person, partly submerged at the water's edge. The feet were above the surface of the water, and one foot was crossed over the other. The body was on its back, with its feet in towards the bank.*

He had gone straight to the police station in Whittlesey and brought to an end a search that had taken squads of police officers with dogs over cold, damp acres and frogmen into the murky waters of fenland

*No parking in Cumbergate now – what remains of it. Most of it has disappeared beneath the Queensgate Shopping Centre.* The author

# MURDER MYSTERY PROBE CONTINUES

## Inquest on farmer is opened and adjourned

### 'APPALLING END' SAYS CORONER

SOME OF THE principal figures in the Farcet Fen murder mystery were present at the inquest on Arthur John Johnson (54), of Crowtree Farm, Farcet, which was opened by the District Coroner, Mr. O. D. G. Barr, of Wisbech, at Whittlesey Town Hall on Tuesday and adjourned for eight weeks.

The witnesses included one of the last persons to see Mr. Johnson alive, Mr. Cyril Kent, of 14, Orchard-street, Peterborough; the man who reported the bachelor farmer's disappearance to the police on Oct. 16th, Mr. C. A. Muncaster, of Woodhall Spa; the angler who discovered the body in Bevill's Leam last Thursday, Mr. M. McCarthy, of 4, Exeter-road, Peterborough; and the police officer in charge of the investigations, Det.-Supt. E. W. Daws, of Scotland Yard's Murder Squad.

After hearing from the Peterborough pathologist, Dr. W. H. Fulton, that Johnson had died as the result of a very extensively fractured skull, the Coroner described his murder as "an appalling end to his life.

Det.-Supt. Daws said it would be quite convenient for him if the inquest was adjourned for eight weeks, and he had no objections to Johnson's funeral taking place as soon as possible.

*Inquest headline: Murder Mystery Probe Continues.* Cambridgeshire Times

drains. At times, mist had come down to shroud the low land and it had been gruelling work.

The last person to see Johnson alive was his friend of thirty years, Cyril Kent. They had met in Peterborough that last evening. He told the inquest that he had gone to the *Greyhound* at nine-fifteen, and Johnson had been there. They had chatted and had a few drinks. They left just after ten, when Clarke had just started pedalling Bessie's bike to Crowtree Farm, and walked to Cumbergate, where Johnson had left his van. He had driven his friend home to Orchard Road.

Kent said: 'My last words to him were, "Cheerio, see you tomorrow." He then drove off towards Farcet Fen.'

Investigations by both the police and the pathologist were still going on, but Dr D H Fulton of Peterborough Memorial Hospital was able to tell the inquest that Johnson's skull, which had a large amount of blood inside it, had five wounds. It had been extensively fractured, the obvious cause of death.

Nothing more could be said at that stage and, adjourning the inquest, the coroner expressed his sympathy with Johnson's relatives and friends 'in this appalling end to his life'.

The police had little to go on beyond a feeling that the killer must have had local knowledge to select such isolated spots to dump both the van and the body. Johnson had been a well-liked man with no enemies and – well – there might be one. A name had been put in the frame by more than one informant. Nobby Clarke.

Clarke had lived and worked at Crowtree Farm. He knew the area. And when it came to a motive he had one – and one to spare.

Friends knew that his marriage was in trouble because he believed Johnson and his wife were having an affair, and he had set off on his way to the farm to 'have it out with him' on the night of the murder. He was also desperately short of money with no hope of clearing his debts.

The police homed in on Clarke's finances.

On 15 October, the day that Johnson had gone missing, that £200 cheque of Clarke's had bounced. On 16 October he was at his bank as soon as it opened and deposited £200 in cash. Later the same day he paid off another debt for £34. Questioned by the police, he said that he had secretly been saving. They found some ten shilling notes in a desk and in his blazer pocket and – they all smelled sort of funny. What was it? Dry rot?

Daws got a search warrant and during the afternoon of 13 November he went through the Clarke home from bottom to top. And in the loft he struck gold. Literally. He found an old purse full of gold sovereigns and half sovereigns. They had belonged to Johnson's mother. And he found £632 in musty notes.

When asked to account for the notes, Clarke, white and shaking, admitted, 'It's Johnson's money.'

Later that evening, at Stanground police station, he confessed to his murder.

A statement made by Clarke was read in court when he appeared before Mr Justice Donovan at Huntingdonshire Assizes in January 1957, pleading not guilty.

*I went to Johnson's place by bike. He came out and met me face to face. He said 'Hello Nobby,' and we talked friendly, and then we got on about him and my wife. He went to hit me and I hit him with something. He pleaded with me to go and talk to him, and I hit him again. I took him to be dead. I sort of panicked at the time and went to get the van from the garage. I was going to put the body in it. I could not find the ignition key and I went back to the body and felt in his pocket for his keys. They were not there and I went into the house.*

He had switched off the radio, taken money from a bureau drawer, and had then found Johnson's bunch of keys, including the safe key, in the kitchen. He said that he had taken money from the safe for revenge.

He had got the body into the van, a sack over the head, and had driven it to Bevill's Leam.

Clarke was found guilty. As Justice Donovan sentenced him to death his advice to him was, 'The circumstances of the crime are so dreadful that you should not count upon another sentence being substituted for the sentence I am about to pass.'

But one was. Clarke was taken to Bedford prison to await execution but on 4 February, just forty-eight hours before he was to be hanged, he was reprieved, an event which caused farm workers in Farcet Fen to stage a protest. They had liked Arthur Johnson. It was the least they could do for him. The last thing.

*Trial headline: Fen Drama Accused Man's Story.* Cambridge Daily News

# FEN DRAMA: ACCUSED MAN'S STORY
## "He Flew for Me: I Hit Him With Wood"
### "YOU HAVE BROKEN UP MY MARRIAGE"

MORRIS ARTHUR CLARKE (27), A LORRY DRIVER, APPEARED BEFORE MR. JUSTICE DONOVAN AGAIN TO-DAY, CHARGED WITH THE MURDER OF A 57-YEAR-OLD FARMER, ARTHUR JOHN JOHNSON, OF FARCET FEN, NEAR PETERBOROUGH.

This is the second day of the trial at Hunts. Assizes.

After a year of his life term in prison, Clarke was allowed to have a pet and, a Cambridgeshire version of *The Birdman of Alcatraz,* he chose a budgie. He was released from prison some years later and, like his budgie, he flew the cage. Where he went to nobody knows.

## Chapter 16

# A Matter of Life and Death
# 1961

Inspector Johnny Walker of Peterborough Combined Police Force was dedicated to his job and to the saving of lives. A married man with three children, he joined the police as a cadet in 1935 and became a constable in 1937. In 1950 he was made a sergeant, and an inspector in 1959.

A familiar tall figure on the streets of Peterborough, he was as well-known for his involvement with Peterborough Swimming Club, where he taught swimming and lifesaving. Chairman of the West Cambridgeshire branch of the Royal Lifesaving Society for many years and holder of the prestigious Royal Humane Society lifesaving award, he became famous in Peterborough for a spectacular series of

*Long Causeway, a bustling Peterborough street.* The author

*The River Nene, Peterborough.* The author

lifesaving successes while carrying out his police duties. They earned him The Queen's Commendation for Bravery twice in three years.

The first time, in 1957, he chased a shopbreaker who jumped into the River Nene and got into difficulties. Walker dived to the rescue – and the arrest. On the next occasion, in 1960, he dived into the Nene again to rescue a small Italian child from the back of a car which had run off the quay near the Customs House. He also rescued his own mother from a gas-filled house.

For someone so devoted to the saving of lives it was perhaps fate at its most cruel that, on Tuesday 24 October 1961, brought him face to face with his own mortality.

He was doing admin work at the police station when word came of a serious incident in Clarence Road. It had begun early that morning when a Soke County Council midwife, Margaret Chapman, had run screaming out into the street.

She had been attending a Yugoslav woman, Milka Kubat, who had given birth to a boy at the house the day before. With a daughter of only eleven months, it had been best for the family for the birth to be at home. And it had been a happy event – until the baby's father, a forty-two-year-old Yugoslav carpenter, Dusan Kubat, had suddenly and savagely attacked Miss Chapman.

In the street, a milkman had taken her to a nearby house and then had called the police. She had multiple bruising and, while the police were on the way, she was taken to Peterborough Memorial

*Clarence Road as it is now.* The author

Hospital. Her injuries were so extensive that relatives later said she was unrecognisable.

When Police Sergeant Percy Vincett went into the house in Clarence Road to question Kubat he found him armed with a seven inch kitchen knife with a pointed blade. He at once attacked Vincett who put an arm protectively across his stomach and was knifed in the left elbow. It was his call for support that took Walker from his desk. He and other officers arrived on the scene shortly before noon.

Kubat was beserk, wielding his knife. Attempts to talk to him and to calm him had no effect. He lunged at Police Constable Reginald Talbot, stabbing him in the ribs, and then Walker felt the knife in his chest.

Other officers, helped by Walker, managed to disarm and arrest Kubat. Only then did Walker collapse, his injury far more serious than he or anyone had realised. He had been stabbed close to the heart. Blood pouring from him, it became an emergency to get him to hospital. With no time to lose waiting for an ambulance, he was hustled into a police car and raced to the hospital where Margaret Chapman was already being treated.

Once there, he insisted on walking in. No stretcher or wheelchair for him. He was strong and fit. But he collapsed. He was, in effect, dying. Unconscious, he was rushed straight to an operating theatre,

*Several houses in Clarence Road, including the one where the stabbing took place, replaced by garages and parking.* The author

where the battle to save his life began, one that, despite the frantic efforts of surgeons and a constant blood transfusion, he seemed to be losing.

His heart had already stopped twice before the emergency operation began. During the operation, it stopped again. Somehow, from somewhere, a priest had been called to give Walker the Last Rites as he lay dying. Walker's wife was at the hospital, no doubt saying prayers of her own. And the answer to someone's prayers somehow became 'not yet, not Johnny Walker'. He was dead, and then the surgeon desperately tried direct heart massage, and it worked. His heart began to beat again, and that time it did not stop.

By eight o'clock that evening he had 'passed the first crisis' and, although sedated, he was able to speak to his wife. A hospital spokesman said: 'He has passed the first hurdle, but his condition is expected to be critical for some days. Luckily, he has a very strong constitution and that seems to have pulled him through.'

Dusan Kubat, with a fawn raincoat over his pyjamas, appeared at a special court at the police station during the afternoon. There was a trickle of blood on his head and face and a wound on the top of his head. Before Councillor J A Savage, he was charged with wounding Inspector Walker with intent to murder him.

His reply was, 'I only can say I want to go in the court.'

'You will get a chance of that,' Councillor Savage assured him.

While Kubat was still muttering about going to court and saying, 'What can I say? What can I say?', he was led away with a police officer holding each arm, supporting him.

He was remanded, while Walker remained critically ill. But after four days his condition was said to be 'very satisfactory,' and he continued to improve. The skill of a surgeon and his own strength and resolution had saved him.

With Kubat later declared insane, Walker soon recovered enough to return to his police work and, eight months later, in June 1962, his bravery was marked by the award of the British Empire Medal.

He retired from the police force in 1967, going on to work as a field officer for the Welland and Nene River Authority, but that moment in Clarence Road, when he had felt the sharpness entering his body, must have stayed with him. The scar was there and, from time to time, some other police officer somewhere in the country would face a similar danger – not always with as fortunate an outcome.

Johnny Walker, who had 'died' on Tuesday 24 October 1961, was given thirty-two more years of life. He died, for the second and last time, in January 1993 at the age of seventy-six.

*A Peterborough police station close to the River Nene.* The author

*Magistrates' Court, Peterborough. The author*

## Chapter 17

# Tigers at Bay
# 1967

About ten-thirty in the evening on 10 March 1967, sixty-two-year-old fen farmer John Robert Auger took his terrier Patsy, for her last walk of the day around The Woodlands, his home in Emneth, near Wisbech.

That walk was the last of all that the two would take together. As he took her back to the shed where she slept, three masked men attacked him. One hit him with a rifle butt, and another with a two foot jemmy, and then he was gagged and tied with rope – unnecessarily, because he was already dying.

His attackers then burst into the living room of the house and trussed and blindfolded Auger's fifty-nine-year-old wife, Isabella, saying, 'If you make a noise we will shoot you.' They said they were from London.

An armed robbery was rare in the Fens, but not so rare was tittle-tattle. In an area where wealth was often measured in acres and yields the gossip was that Auger was a wealthy man in the more usual sense of the word and there had been two recent attempted robberies at The Woodlands.

That third one succeeded. They took Auger's safe. It was heavy but they managed to get it outside and drive off with it in his green VW pick-up.

Audrey, the Augers' daughter, arrived home soon after to discover her mother in a faint, but unhurt. Auger was dead when they found him, his skull split to the brain.

Cambridgeshire police immediately called in Norfolk Constabulary CID. The farm was near the county boundary and the killers could have crossed it, but the investigation was to be led by Detective Superintendent Wallace Virgo of Scotland Yard.

It was known at once that the three were not from London. They had not fooled Isabella. She said: 'They had local voices.' And people in the area, although many were afraid to 'copper' on the gang, could put names to them. When fenland lads went badly wrong they tended to be noticed and everyone, including the police, knew those responsible.

All three, although still in their twenties, already had many convictions and had spent time in prison. In a matter of days they were arrested – one at home, one in a Wisbech betting shop and one trying to crawl under a double-bed in Birmingham. Charged with breaking and entering The Woodlands and murdering Auger were Patrick Joseph Collins of no fixed abode, Graham Warden of Wisbech, and Barrie Paul Cooper of Sutton St Edmund.

Cooper, the son of highly respectable parents, a headteacher and a postmaster, was the leader of the gang. At twenty-five, he was a seasoned housebreaker who had committed sixty thefts in six months. He was proud of his 'technique' and his ability to quickly fence stolen goods, but experience had not given him discernment.

The word had been that Auger was wealthy. After killing him, Cooper had led his associates straight to the safe, later found, forced open, in a bramble bush a few miles away. Old, its key lost for two years, it had contained only four shillings. Auger's wealth had not been there. He had been killed for what, today, would not buy a packet of crisps.

Perhaps the young fen tigers cannot be blamed for their ignorance. It was, after all, before the antiques valuation programmes on television. There was no *Antiques Roadshow*. They knew about silver, and had stolen it in the past, but – Staffordshire? And Dresden? Manhandling that safe, they had made their big mistake. They had ignored Auger's collection of china, the finest in East Anglia, now valued at over £1,000,000.

Their trial opened before Mr Justice Glyn Jones at Hertfordshire Assizes on 27 June 1967 with prosecutor Owen Stable saying that the crime was of hideous proportions. Auger had been attacked with 'demoniacal savagery' and had appalling injuries. The gang had been vicious and ruthless and had gone to the farm 'armed to the teeth'.

Isabella Auger gave evidence, but then, unexpectedly, attention began to centre on the police. As the trial continued, serious allegations of corruption and conspiracy would be made against many of the officers involved in the case, all of whom had made written notes of interviews and conversations with the accused. Most of them were challenged by the three defence counsels. Such was the time taken with allegations and counter-allegations that Glyn Jones remarked that it was 'a great pity' that the police were not provided with tape recorders.

Contention began on the second day of the trial. Detective Inspector Leonard Trevor, a Wisbech-based crime squad officer who knew Cooper as a thief and had interviewed him at home for four hours, was called upon to deny putting pressure on him by saying, 'If you don't make a statement to me I'll get Superintendent Virgo and the police to come here with sirens going. How would the kids at your mother's school like that?'

Collins, from under the bed, had been escorted, pale and with his knees trembling and hands shaking, to King's Lynn to say to Virgo, 'You have got the other two. I was expecting this. I was there, but I didn't do the thumping. If you write that down I shall strongly deny any charge of murder. I've got to look after myself.'

By the time he came to court, his defence, James Comyn, was complaining about police behaviour. His client had only said that to Virgo because he had been threatened on the journey to King's Lynn. Detective Sergeant Grant had said: 'You'd better co-operate with us. If you co-operate we'll get you off with five years. Otherwise we'll get you life.'

Comyn then accused Virgo, who had been told the height of the men by Isabella, of making his client fit. He had been heard to say, 'He's a bit too tall, but he'll have to do.' That would not do, Comyn said.

Virgo remained under fire. Leslie Boreham, for Warden, said that he had fabricated a remark, said to have been made by Warden, that, 'Even if you are from the Yard you wont prove anything. I was in it but there was nothing left behind and you know it.' Virgo responded with, 'I am appalled at this suggestion and deny the whole thing.'

The remark was crucial. It proved that Warden had been at The Woodlands. His later withdrawal was really no surprise to Virgo. All three men were professional criminals, fen tigers full of fight, and not even the best of Scotland Yard, a future head of the Flying Squad, could cow them. He had been forewarned of what might happen when Collins had said, when interviewed, 'If you write that down I'll say you verballed me.'

The prosecution called fifty witnesses, many very afraid of the three in the dock. Two were so scared that they did a runner, never to be seen again. Allegations against the police continued, but the real business of the trial had to go on.

Cooper offered an alibi. He had been in Wisbech. On the evening of the murder, he had a drink with Warden in the *Bowling Green* pub in Lynn Road and had then spent an hour at the fair before making his way to Palmer's garage in Lynn Road. He had reached it over gardens at the back and intended to steal 5,000 cigarettes, but he

*The* Bowling Green, *Lynn Road, Wisbech.* The author

could not force the door and the windows were barred. When a car
had come he had run away. Four people swore that he was at a house
in Beatrice Road at nine-thirty. All later changed their minds.

Stable told Cooper: 'You are an idle layabout, driving about in your
van, drinking, betting and sitting about in cafes.' Cooper agreed.

In his alibi he had mentioned intending to steal 5,000 cigarettes.
To discount that, Stable had 5,000 brought into court from a nearby
shop, stacking carton after carton on the witness box. If he had
succeeded, how, he was asked, would he have carried them away over
a six foot fence and several gardens? No thief in his right mind would
try to break into Palmer's. Cooper's instant response was, 'It depends
how the mind thinks.'

A day in Warden's life was said to be much the same as Cooper's.
They backed horses at the same bookies, drank at the same pub,
the *Bowling Green*, and talked in the same cafes. Neither worked.
Warden had been an industrial painter but he had given that up to live
off 'savings and gambling'. And, like Cooper, he said that he was the
victim of a police conspiracy. He had not made the admissions
claimed and had not been at The Woodlands when Auger had been
murdered.

When Stable accused him of living off the proceeds of crime, he
said: 'No sir, the only job I've done is the turkeys. To get a Christmas
dinner.' He was, at that time, in jail for attempting to steal turkeys in
Suffolk.

And on the night of the murder? Nowhere near. He had been with Cooper in Wisbech but, at about nine o'clock, he had felt ill and had gone to his mother's in Bath Road. At midnight he had gone home to Guild Road, and his girlfriend. He added: 'Before Christmas I was nearly an alcoholic and I still suffer with my stomach.' And, of the Auger crime: 'It was nothing to do with me. Whatever my mates do I've got no sympathy with them.'

So that left Collins to have his say, the only one of the three to admit being at The Woodlands. Or had he? He had form, and a false bank account in Spalding. He had broken into twelve shops and offices in eight months and, in 1964, he had escaped from police custody. Disguised with a beard and glasses, he had gone on the run. Now, on trial for Auger's murder, it was his turn to deny all the admissions he was alleged to have made, including the bit about not doing the thumping.

It had been a police set-up, he claimed. Virgo had told Detective Sergeant Barry what to write and, Collins said, 'There wasn't a lot I could do. When I said I never said anything Virgo told me to shut up.'

At last, the trial neared its turbulent end. On 12 July the jury heard the closing speeches of prosecution and defence, and, according to Cooper's defence, Hugh Griffiths QC, it had all been about rumour, speculation and police procedure when the facts were that his client was 'a petty, miserable thief' but not a violent man. He was 'about as miserable a parasite on society as you could expect to find in a month of Sundays,' but he had nothing to do with Auger's murder.

Would the jury agree?

Summing up the next day, Glyn Jones queried the defence allegations that the police had invented oral admissions. The trial had been so muddied by claims and counter-claims for and against the police that the entire proceedings had been in danger of becoming a fiasco. He had kept control, but he had had to work hard to do so. All involved were distressed at the way things had gone.

On that last day, Comyn, perhaps, spoke for everyone when he said:

*I hope if this case establishes anything it will be to get rid of oral admissions, and I hope we will have some untamperable means of court recording in the future. This sort of nonsense has gone on long enough and the police oral evidence in this case is all there is. We have to be careful about the police going into the witness box and saying, 'He admitted it to me. I am an honourable man.' We would be coming to the stage when a defendant would be damned before he started.*

## Summing up in Fen murder trial

# Judge queries 'corruption' allegations against police

SERIOUS allegations of corruption and conspiracy made against the police, were queried by the Fenland murder trial judge yesterday afternoon.

Summing up on the twelfth day of the trial at Hertford Assizes, Mr Justice Glyn-Jones asked the jury: "What would be easier for these 'wicked' policemen than to put soil from near the murdered man's body on to the three men's clothing?"

He said there had been no attempt to contaminate the clothing with fake physical evidence taken from John Robert Auger's Emneth farm.

Defence counsel for each accused—Barrie Paul Cooper, David Graham Warden and Patrick Joseph Collins — all suggested that police invented alleged oral admissions.

The judge said that however many men were in the gang — it has been hinted that there were five — they left the Woodlands on March 18 "panic-stricken, knowing that what started out as a robbery had ended in a murder".

*Trial Account: Judge queries 'corruption' allegations against the police.* Peterborough Telegraph

The jury, obliged to sit through it all, found all three men not guilty of murder but guilty of manslaughter. An emotionless Cooper was jailed for fifteen years and Warden and Collins each got twelve years.

Before the trial, Patsy, Auger's adored terrier who had been with him on that last walk, a dumb witness, was gently put to sleep. She was very old and infirm and Auger had been thinking, sadly, that it was time for her to go.

As it had turned out, he had been the one to go, but not gently.

## Chapter 18

# A Cotton Wool World
# 1972

embers of the Royal Family were enjoying the Christmas season at Sandringham, so the front page of the *Lynn News and Advertiser* for Tuesday 2 January 1973 featured that. Over three thousand people had come to see them arrive at church for morning service on the last day of the old year and to listen to the relayed sermon by the Bishop of Norwich who, as a Canaries fan, slipped in a forecast that Norwich City would beat Chelsea 2-1 to reach the League Cup final at Wembley.

Their walk back to Sandringham was a sight worth waiting for that chill morning. The Queen wore red, Princess Anne blue and the Queen Mother fur-trimmed black and white. There was applause, cheering and the click of camera shutters.

A small item at the foot of that page seemed almost overwhelmed. It could have been missed, but for the starkness of its headline:

*BOY FOUND ASPHYXIATED MOTHER REMANDED ON MURDER CHARGE*

The murdered boy was Simon Geoffrey Bushell and his mother was Margaret Bushell. They lived in Downham Market, a small town beside the Great Ouse as it flowed on to King's Lynn. In the heart of fenland, it was an almost insular community where family was important.

Margaret, a divorcee, had come to Downham from her native Manchester in 1953, bringing with her her two young children, Denise and Terry. She became housekeeper to Sidney Bushell, a billposter with British Railways and conductor of a local brass band, twenty-one years her senior, and they soon married and began to raise a family of their own. They would have five children together.

In 1972, Sidney having died from cancer in 1968, Margaret shared her council house on the Retreat Estate, one in a small terrace of four,

*Retreat Estate street sign, Downham Market.* The author

with two of their children, fourteen year old Jane and seven year old Simon.

She doted on them, especially Simon. Her world revolved around him. And Terry, then twenty-seven, loved him too. He would often

*Restreat Estate, Downham Market.* The author

*Restreat Estate, Downham Market.* The author

pick him up from Wimbotsham Primary School, where he was considered 'backward,' when Margaret was working.

All had seemed well on Christmas Day 1972. Terry, with his wife and baby, visited the Bushell family during the morning of Christmas

*Shopping for Christmas turkeys, Downham Market.* The author

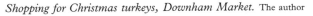

*Christmas trees for sale, Downham Market.* The author

Day. They were living in Stow Bardolph while they looked for a house in Downham. Everything was fine. Everyone was happy. Margaret later said:

> *We had got everything – a Christmas tree with lights, decorations, all the Christmas food, presents, and a bottle of wine my boss had given me.*

She worked for a taxi firm and for a cafe. Always a hard worker, she had not been feeling too well. She had been overdoing things. She had seen Dr Johnson, who had prescribed the tranquiliser Librium, one three times a day, and the sleeping tablet Mogadon, one at night. She was told that they were very mild. Really, besides being over-worked, she was stressed.

Simon was getting her down. The focus of her life, his every move was noticed and analyzed, and it worried her intensely that he had nervous habits.

They had begun before he had started school. He kept wiping his nose on a hankie and on his sleeve. He put his fingers up his nose and twitched his nose, he blinked a lot, and he shook his head. Lately, he had begun to rub one foot against the other trouser leg. Shortly before Christmas, he had gone swimming and the other boys had made fun of his nose twitching. It had distressed her.

She had been so upset that, on 19 December, she had spoken to Dr Johnson about him, saying that he made her 'all worked up'. She was told that the pills would calm her, but they didn't.

By 23 December she had become so agitated that she phoned the doctor's surgery again and spoke to Dr Malcolm, a locum. 'He said a lot of children do things like that and to pretend I hadn't seen him doing it.' He said that if she was still worried after Christmas she was to bring him in.

She wanted to take him that day but she had been working. 'I had Simon on my mind all the time. I was ever so worried about him.' And there would not be another surgery until after Boxing Day.

And so, Christmas Day had come, and her visitors, and everything was fine, but – 'I was getting all worked up but I didn't want them to know and tried not to show it.' She had bounced her baby grand-daughter on her knee and everything had been fine.

After Terry had gone, Margaret, Jane and Simon had lunch, and then they watched television. 'Simon was playing with all his new toys. But all the time I was getting all worked up because he was twitching his nose and shaking his head.' He had known that his mother was watching him, although as she had been advised, she pretended to ignore him.

At seven-thirty, Simon was put to bed. He had wanted to take all his new toys up with him but was allowed to take only his favourite, a digger. He went to bed after being given two of his mother's Mogadon tablets. Since getting the prescription, she had been giving Simon Mogadon and Librium to help him to sleep.

At eight-thirty she and Jane, who knew nothing of her mother's concerns about Simon, heard 'crash-bang noises' from upstairs. The digger being thrown on the floor. Margaret went up and told him to stop being naughty and to go to sleep. She took the digger away.

Jane went to bed at nine and it was after that, as she was reading, that Margaret heard another noise from Simon's room:

*I thought he had gone to sleep. I sat on the settee. I was getting all worked up and I think I took a Mogadon to quieten me down. All of a sudden I heard Simon again. From what I could hear he was running around his bedroom making playing noises.*

It was after midnight by then. Boxing Day. To settle him, she took him a hot water bottle, and then, as she was on her way downstairs, she heard him making noises again:

*I turned round and ran upstairs. I was in such a state. I don't know whether I gave him the Mogadon or if I took it myself. Everything was beginning to go round. I couldn't see Simon or anyone, but I knew Simon was there. After giving him the tablets I started to go downstairs and he began shouting. Everything seemed to get on top of me and I had reached the end of my tether. I went upstairs, grabbed a pillow, and held it over his face for a few minutes. He did not make any more noises. I thought he was dead when I took it off his face.*

She had remembered more of what had happened by the time she was put on trial for murder at Norwich Crown Court in May 1973, although David Hunter QC, prosecuting, found her account 'rather bizarre' and said that she was shutting out what really happened.

In a soft voice to a hushed court, she said:

*I seemed to be in a dream, a haze. Everything seemed to be a long way off. There were all kinds of flashing coloured lights in front of my eyes, my ears were pumping, and everything was a cotton wool world. If I had realised I was hurting him I would not have done it as I loved him so much. I just wanted to frighten him, to stop him making a noise. Suddenly I was looking at his hand and it just dropped. It had only taken a second.*

In the early hours of Boxing Day, Margaret's phone calls had brought the doctor and the police to her home on the Retreat Estate. Efforts were made to revive Simon, but to no avail. Margaret was arrested and taken to Downham police station. She had already confessed to killing Simon to Detective Chief Inspector Charles Nourse, the head of Lynn CID, and at five in the morning she confessed again in a statement.

In the old Castle Assizes courtroom, she seemed an unlikely murderess. But most of them do. She was an ordinary forty-nine-year-old widow and mother, neatly dressed in an imitation leopard skin coat, calmly facing the consequences of having got all worked up with her little boy, sleepless after an exciting Christmas Day.

Terry said that she had been a good mother and worshipped Simon, spoiling him, and yet, on her own admission, she had killed him – without meaning to. Hunter doubted that. He said: 'It is an unpleasant story with only one answer – she intended to do what she did and was aware of the inevitability of the consequences.' He said that, in the witness box, she had revealed herself as a person wholly capable of suffocating her son with a pillow and resorting to untruths to escape her obvious guilt. 'From start to finish she retained a quite remarkable composure and you may think that she showed very little remorse indeed and very little distress.' Simon had been playing with his toys. Hunter's opinion was: 'The population would be decimated if this behaviour justified or excused what happened to this small boy.'

It was an upsetting trial for all concerned. Trials involving the death of a child always were. Worst of all was the outcome of the post-mortem on Simon's body. A pathologist said that Simon had inhaled vomit which had caused asphyxia. A forensic scientist, who had examined the stomach contents, said that Simon had been given at least five Librium and six Mogadon tablets which could have contributed to his death, causing shortage of oxygen.

Mr Justice Caulfield summed up for five hours, his gentle opening remarks expressing the feelings of the court. 'Most of you no doubt equate Christmas Day with a birth rather than a death, with joy rather than with sadness, with an affectionate mother rather than a cold one, and you may think of a crib rather than a coffin.' But then he got to his instructions to the jury. Efforts had been made to create a dispassionate atmosphere in court and they were to remember that and not succumb to the 'big temptation' of settling for the compromise of manslaughter. Michael Self, defending Margaret would have had them go even further. He had asked for an acquittal.

Tempted or not, the jury found it difficult to reach a verdict. After six and a half hours, Caulfield sent word that he would accept a majority decision. And, after more than seven hours, that is what he got. With a pregnant woman juror in tears, Margaret was found guilty of murdering Simon by an eleven to one majority.

Sentencing her to life imprisonment, Caulfield, as affected as everyone in court, said: 'I do not think it appropriate that I should pass any comment.' Quietly, almost as if she was not there, Margaret Bushell was led away.

But that was not the end of the Margaret Bushell story.

By the next morning, her full story, its details sensationalised, was filling the tabloids, and, unrevealed while she had been standing trial, what a full story it was. Of the five children born to her and Sidney only Jane remained alive. Simon had been murdered by his mother, but – what had happened to the other three?

Let's begin with Cheryl Diana. In March 1958, at the age of three, she had been found face down in six inches of water and bleach in the bath. Margaret had popped next door, just for a moment, and when she had come back she had found the little girl dead. Inquest verdict: Accidental death.

Next – Stephen. Only six weeks after the death of Cheryl, Stephen had died on his fifth birthday. After a supper treat of tomato ketchup sandwiches he, unlike Simon, had gone happily to bed. The next morning he had been found on the concrete path, twelve feet below his bedroom window, his neck broken. A doctor confirmed that he sleepwalked. Inquest verdict: Death by misadventure.

The Bushells were given the kindest support in Downham. Losing one child was bad enough, but to lose two in such tragic circumstances – nothing could be worse. Could it?

But what about Timothy? Twenty months later, in January 1960, three year old Timothy had drowned in the clothes boiler. Sidney had been childminding while Margaret was at work, watching Saturday afternoon racing on the television with Jane on his knee. It got cold and dark, but he did not check on Timothy. When Margaret came home she went into the washhouse and there was Timothy, head down in seven inches of water.

For a third time coroner Arthur Bantoft was called upon to conduct an inquest into the death of a Bushell child. Verdict: Accidental death.

Support for the Bushells was by then a little more guarded. The deaths had been no more than sickening coincidence, but doubts began to be raised of their fitness to be parents. The Bushells themselves blamed bad luck.

Sidney said: 'We must be one of the unluckiest families in the country. I think there's a jinx on us or on this house.'

Margaret said: 'We've never had anything but bad luck since we moved here seven years ago.'

They said that, to change their luck, they were going to move. 'We can't stand another tragedy in this family.'

But it had been difficult to find an exchange council house and they had stayed. Sidney had died from cancer, and still the bad luck was there on the Retreat Estate. One more child was to die.

As the story was making headline news, the area MPs called for an inquiry, a fresh look into those earlier deaths. Paul Hawkins and Dr Tom Stuttaford said that the matter should be raised with the Home Secretary, Robert Carr.

But the obvious first person to comment on the deaths of Cheryl, Stephen and Timothy was Arthur Bantoft, recently retired. He said that the police had investigated each death at the time and had been satisfied that they had been accidents but, in over twenty years as a coroner, it had been the only case of that kind that he had been involved in. He called the Bushells' losses 'extraordinary'.

After Margaret's conviction for Simon's murder and the renewed furore as to the actual nature of those three earlier deaths, the police came under fire. They stuck to their findings as staunchly as Bantoft. There had been no evidence to indicate that they had been anything but unfortunate accidents. There were no known grounds for re-opening those cases but, due to Hawkins' pressure on the Home Secretary, Norfolk Constabulary was ordered to do so.

A senior police officer new to the cases was appointed to lead the investigations. Verdict: The verdicts at the times of the deaths had been correct. The Bushells had just been, as Sidney had said, one of the unluckiest families in the country.

The final end to the Margaret Bushell story.

# Select Bibliography

**Books and Journals**

Abbott, Geoffrey *William Calcraft, Executioner Extra-ordinaire*, Eric Dobby Publishing, Broadstairs, 2004

Abbott, Geoffrey *Execution: A Guide to the Ultimate Penalty*, Summerdale, Chichester, 2005

Bell, John *Cambridgeshire Crimes*, Popular Publications, St Ives, 1994

Bell, John *More Crimes of Cambridgeshire*, Popular Publications, St Ives, 1995

Bennett, Stewart *A History of Lincolnshire*, Phillimore, Chichester, 1999

Berridge, Virginia 'Opium and Oral History', *Journal of the Oral History Society*, volume 7, number 2, Autumn 1979, 48–58

Berridge, Virginia and Griffith, Edward *Opium and the People*, Yale University Press, New Haven, 1987

Bevis, Trevor *Mini Stories from the Fens*, The Author, 1992

Blakeman, Pamela *Ely Prisons*, Ely Society, Ely, 2001

Brooks, Pamela *Ghastly True Tales of the Norfolk Poisoners*, Halsgrove, Wellington, 2007

Bruce, Alison *Cambridgeshire Murders*, Sutton, Stroud, 2003

Butcher, Brian David *A Movable Rambling Police: An Official History of Policing in Norfolk*, Norfolk Constabulary, Norwich, 1989

Clark, Ross *Cambridgeshire*, Random House, London, 1996

Defoe, Daniel 'Tour Through the Eastern Counties', *East Anglian Magazine*, Ipswich, 1984

Downham Market and District Amenity Society *A History of Downham Market*, 1999

Farrell, Michael *Poisons and Poisoners*, Robert Hale, London, 1992

Fielding, Steve *The Executioner's Bible: The Story of Every Hangman of the Twentieth Century*, John Blake Publishing, London, 2007

Gash, Norman *Mr Secretary Peel*, Longmans, London, 1961

Gerrard, Valerie *The Story of the Fens*, Robert Hale, London, 2003

Humphreys, Sir Travers *A Book of Trials*, Heinemann, London, 1953

Klein, Leonora *A Very English Hangman: The Life and Times of Albert Pierrepoint*, Corvo, London, 2006

Lane, Brian *The Encyclopaedia of Forensic Science*, Headline, London, 1993

Latham, Robert and Matthews, William (eds) *The Diary of Samuel Pepys Volume IV*, Bell, London, 1972

Morris, Christopher (ed) *The Journeys of Celia Fiennes*, Cresset Press, London, 1947

Peacock, A J *Bread or Blood*, Victor Gollanz, London, 1965

Richings, Derek and Rudderham, Roger *Strange Tales of East Anglia*, SB Publications, Seaford, 1998

Ruderham (misprint for Rudderham), Roger *Littleport Chronicle 1770–1899. Some Extracts from the Cambridge Chronicle*, Standard Project, Wisbech, 1981

Storey, Edward *The Winter Fens*, Robert Hale, London, 1993

Thurlow, David *The Norfolk Nightmare*, Robert Hale, London, 1993

Thurlow, David *Evil in East Anglia*, Robert Hale, London, 1993

West, H Mills *East Anglian Yarns*, Countryside, Newbury, 1992

Young, Hugh *My Forty Years at the Yard*, WH Allen, London, 1955

**Newspapers**

*Cambridge Chronicle*
*Cambridge Daily News*
*Cambridge Evening News*
*Cambridge Independent Press*
*Cambridgeshire Times*
*Daily Express*
*Daily Mail*
*Ely Standard*
*Ely Standard and Cambridgeshire Times*
*Lincoln, Rutland and Stamford Mercury*
*Lynn News and Advertiser*
*Market Rasen Mail*
*Morning Chronicle*
*Norwich Mercury*
*Peterborough Advertiser*
*Peterborough Evening Telegraph*
*Peterborough Standard*
*Wisbech Advertiser*

# TRUE CRIME FROM WHARNCLIFFE

*Foul Deeds and Suspicious Deaths Series*

# OTHER TRUE CRIME BOOKS FROM WHARNCLIFFE

*Please contact us via any of the methods below for more information
or a catalogue*
WHARNCLIFFE BOOKS
47 Church Street, Barnsley, South Yorkshire, S70 2AS
Tel: 01226 734555 • 734222 • Fax: 01226 734438
email: enquiries@pen-and-sword.co.uk
website: www.wharncliffebooks.co.uk

# Index